OPPOSING VIEWPOINTS®

Sex

Other Books of Related Interest

OPPOSING VIEWPOINTS®

Sex

Mary E. Williams, *Book Editor*

David L. Bender, *Publisher*
Bruno Leone, *Executive Editor*
Bonnie Szumski, *Editorial Director*
David M. Haugen, *Managing Editor*

OPPOSING
VIEWPOINTS®
SERIES

Greenhaven Press, Inc., San Diego, California

Cover photo: John Foxx Images/Planet Art

Library of Congress Cataloging-in-Publication Data

Sex : opposing viewpoints / Mary E. Williams, book editor.
     p.   cm. — (Opposing viewpoints series)
   Includes bibliographical references and index.
    ISBN 0-7377-0352-0 (lib. : alk. paper). —
  ISBN 0-7377-0351-2 (pbk. : alk. paper)
    1. Sex—United States. 2. Sexual ethics—United States. 3. Sex
customs—United States. I. Williams, Mary E., 1960–   . II. Series:
Opposing viewpoints series (Unnumbered)

HQ18.U5 S484 2000
306.7—dc21   99-059374
                                                      CIP

Greenhaven Press, Inc., P.O. Box 289009
San Diego, CA 92198-9009

"Congress shall make
no law...abridging the
freedom of speech, or of
the press."

First Amendment to the U.S. Constitution

The basic foundation of our democracy is the First
Amendment guarantee of freedom of expression. The
Opposing Viewpoints Series is dedicated to the
concept of this basic freedom and the idea that it is
more important to practice it than to enshrine it.

Contents

Why Consider Opposing Viewpoints?

"The only way in which a human being can make some approach to knowing the whole of a subject is by hearing what can be said about it by persons of every variety of opinion and studying all modes in which it can be looked at by every character of mind. No wise man ever acquired his wisdom in any mode but this."

John Stuart Mill

In our media-intensive culture it is not difficult to find differing opinions. Thousands of newspapers and magazines and dozens of radio and television talk shows resound with differing points of view. The difficulty lies in deciding which opinion to agree with and which "experts" seem the most credible. The more inundated we become with differing opinions and claims, the more essential it is to hone critical reading and thinking skills to evaluate these ideas. Opposing Viewpoints books address this problem directly by presenting stimulating debates that can be used to enhance and teach these skills. The varied opinions contained in each book examine many different aspects of a single issue. While examining these conveniently edited opposing views, readers can develop critical thinking skills such as the ability to compare and contrast authors' credibility, facts, argumentation styles, use of persuasive techniques, and other stylistic tools. In short, the Opposing Viewpoints Series is an ideal way to attain the higher-level thinking and reading skills so essential in a culture of diverse and contradictory opinions.

In addition to providing a tool for critical thinking, Opposing Viewpoints books challenge readers to question their own strongly held opinions and assumptions. Most people form their opinions on the basis of upbringing, peer pressure, and personal, cultural, or professional bias. By reading carefully balanced opposing views, readers must directly confront new ideas as well as the opinions of those with whom they disagree. This is not to simplisti-cally argue that everyone who reads opposing views will—or should—change his or her opinion. Instead, the series enhances readers' understanding of their own views by encouraging confrontation with opposing ideas. Care-ful examination of others' views can lead to the readers' understanding of the logical inconsistencies in their own opinions, perspective on why they hold an opinion, and the consideration of the possibility that their opinion re-quires further evaluation.

Evaluating Other Opinions

To ensure that this type of examination occurs, Opposing Viewpoints books present all types of opinions. Prominent spokespeople on different sides of each issue as well as well-known professionals from many disciplines challenge the reader. An additional goal of the series is to provide a forum for other, less known, or even unpopular viewpoints. The opinion of an ordinary person who has had to make the de-cision to cut off life support from a terminally ill relative, for example, may be just as valuable and provide just as much insight as a medical ethicist's professional opinion. The editors have two additional purposes in including these less known views. One, the editors encourage readers to re-spect others' opinions—even when not enhanced by profes-sional credibility. It is only by reading or listening to and objectively evaluating others' ideas that one can determine whether they are worthy of consideration. Two, the inclu-sion of such viewpoints encourages the important critical thinking skill of objectively evaluating an author's creden-tials and bias. This evaluation will illuminate an author's reasons for taking a particular stance on an issue and will aid in readers' evaluation of the author's ideas.

As series editors of the Opposing Viewpoints Series, it is our hope that these books will give readers a deeper under-standing of the issues debated and an appreciation of the complexity of even seemingly simple issues when good and honest people disagree. This awareness is particularly im-portant in a democratic society such as ours in which people enter into public debate to determine the common good.

Those with whom one disagrees should not be regarded as enemies but rather as people whose views deserve careful examination and may shed light on one's own.

Thomas Jefferson once said that "difference of opinion leads to inquiry, and inquiry to truth." Jefferson, a broadly educated man, argued that "if a nation expects to be ignorant and free . . . it expects what never was and never will be." As individuals and as a nation, it is imperative that we consider the opinions of others and examine them with skill and discernment. The Opposing Viewpoints Series is intended to help readers achieve this goal.

David L. Bender & Bruno Leone,
Series Editors

Greenhaven Press anthologies primarily consist of previously published material taken from a variety of sources, including periodicals, books, scholarly journals, newspapers, government documents, and position papers from private and public organizations. These original sources are often edited for length and to ensure their accessibility for a young adult audience. The anthology editors also change the original titles of these works in order to clearly present the main thesis of each viewpoint and to explicitly indicate the opinion presented in the viewpoint. These alterations are made in consideration of both the reading and comprehension levels of a young adult audience. Every effort is made to ensure that Greenhaven Press accurately reflects the original intent of the authors included in this anthology.

Introduction

"Sexuality has become a pawn in power struggles between competing political interest groups."

—Pepper Schwartz and Virginia Rutter

In her book *Slut!: Growing Up Female with a Bad Reputation*, Leora Tanenbaum decries the societal message that adolescent girls often receive—that only bad, "slutty" women have sexual desires. Conversely, Wendy Shalit, author of *A Return to Modesty*, maintains that teenagers' discomfort with sexuality is an "instinctive," protective mechanism that can help youths avoid premature sexual relations. In a July 1999 *Salon* magazine article featuring a debate between these two authors, Tanenbaum asserts that "girls *and* boys" should learn that "sexual desire is a natural part of adolescence" lest they end up feeling "guilty and ashamed of their own sexual desire." Shalit counters that "girls are then more vulnerable because they don't have . . . embarrassment to protect them."

This disagreement between Shalit and Tanenbaum mirrors a larger conflict in society concerning the liberal sexual ideals that first gained wide acceptance in the 1960s. These ideals—particularly the acceptance of nonmarital sex and open attitudes toward sexuality—are being challenged by those who advocate more conservative approaches to sexual issues. Debate remains fierce over whether sexual liberation or restraint serves society best.

Much of this debate focuses on the sexual revolution—the radical transformation of sexual attitudes and mores that began in the 1960s—and its effect on women. As its defenders point out, the sexual revolution expanded women's options regarding sex. The advent of the birth control pill increased female access to contraception, and this, in conjunction with the women's rights movement, afforded women more control over their sexual lives. Meanwhile, societal censure of nonmarital sex and cohabitation decreased. By the mid-1970s, a pregnant, unmarried woman could either have an abortion or opt for single motherhood—with less stigma attached to both—and feel less obligated to enter into an unwanted marriage. As author Lillian B. Rubin writes, "Women, reveling in their newfound liberation, sought the sexual freedom that had been for so long 'for men only.'"

But many believe that the sexual revolution has come at too high a cost. According to National Public Radio commentator Frederica Mathewes-Green, "the negative fallout has been hard to ignore: divorce, disease, abortion, illegitimacy, and multiplying heartbreak." Moreover, Mathewes-Green argues, as societal acceptance of sex without commitment has increased, the possibilities for committed, genuinely loving relationships between young men and women have decreased: "If girls give sex to get love, while boys give love in order to get sex, dumping free sex on the market inevitably drove the cost of love through the roof. Female bargaining power was demolished. Girls had to fling enormous quantities of sex at boys in desperate attempts to buy the smallest units of love." Sexual liberation, many observers contend, has left women embittered by the lack of depth and intimacy in their lives and men emotionally isolated and detached from relationships and family life.

This growing disillusionment with casual sex—intensified by high divorce rates and the fear of sexually transmitted diseases—has started to produce "more cautious, conservative attitudes among the young," maintains syndicated columnist John Leo. "Support for premarital sex remains high, but it dropped from 80 percent in 1988 to 71 percent in 1995," Leo reports. Moreover, he points out, teen sexual activity, as well as teen pregnancy, is on the decrease. Anti-promiscuity messages are on the rise—from revised sex education curricula that promote sexual abstinence to self-help books such as Ellen Fein and Sherrie Schneider's *The Rules: Time-Tested Secrets for Capturing the Heart of Mr. Right*. Increasingly, religious and political conservatives are stressing the importance of abstinence among singles and heterosexual monogamy among married couples, proclaiming that only these forms of sexual conduct create healthy families and stable societies.

Many progressives grant that the sexual revolution has contributed to the creation of a "hypersexualized" society.

They lament, for example, the exploitation of sexuality seen in advertising and in the entertainment industry. As Sarah van Gelder, executive director of the Positive Futures Network, writes: "The mysteries of sexual ecstasy are trivialized—all is laid out in magazines and videos. There is little discussion of the effects of inundating the culture with superficial images of sexuality and associating those images with consumerism, violence, and exploitation rather than love and creativity." An aversion to commercialized "valueless" sexuality, van Gelder contends, causes some people to seek the safety of clearly defined, traditional values that emphasize monogamous heterosexual marriage as the norm.

Some liberals and feminists, however, maintain that the backlash against sexual liberation is really a backlash against female independence. In their book *The Gender of Sexuality*, Pepper Schwartz and Virginia Rutter contend that today's conservative activists wish to "browbeat women back into traditional incarnations of womanhood by resurrecting the flagging double standard." For instance, Schwartz and Rutter argue, conservatives who disapprove of out-of-wedlock births may denounce "all those who have sex outside of marriage. But because women bear children, they are easier targets of scandal and criticism than are men." An example of this can be seen in the 1996 arrest of an unmarried pregnant nineteen-year-old in Boise, Idaho. In an attempt to stem the tide of unwed pregnancies, the town had decided to enforce its old laws against fornication: The woman was placed on probation and required to do community service for engaging in nonmarital sex. The police targeted her because they had been told to seek out women with "big bellies and no wedding rings." Such a policy, Schwartz and Rutter point out, winks at unwed sex among males while punishing women for the same behavior. Although the Idaho case is unusual, these authors maintain, it is indicative of a more widespread desire to limit women's sexual autonomy.

To thwart such double standards, many policymakers stress the need for Americans to become more educated about sexuality so that they can approach the traditionally taboo subject from a reasonable perspective. The Sexuality Information and Education Council of the United States

(SIECUS), for example, contends that increased access to information about sexuality helps people take responsibility for their own attitudes and behavior. In SIECUS's view, sexually informed adults "engage in sexual relationships that are consensual, nonexploitative, honest, pleasurable, and protected against disease and unintended pregnancy." Moreover, such individuals "demonstrate respect for people with different sexual values."

Whether the U.S. can resolve its conflicts over sexuality remains to be seen. For now, the forces of both sexual liberation and restraint continue to mold sexual ideals, and the legacy of the sexual revolution remains controversial. The authors in *Sex: Opposing Viewpoints* debate some of the most contentious issues concerning sexuality in the following chapters: What Is the State of Sexual Ethics in America? What Sexual Behaviors Should Society Promote? How Should Sex Education Be Conducted? Are Some Sexual Practices Unacceptable? Sexual attitudes and behavior in the United States have changed dramatically in recent decades. How these values continue to shift will play an important role in shaping society in the future.

CHAPTER 1

What Is the State of Sexual Ethics in America?

Chapter Preface

In 1998, President Bill Clinton's confession that he had had an "inappropriate relationship" of a sexual nature with White House intern Monica Lewinsky started a national discussion about how a politician's personal moral standards might affect his or her ability to lead. Clinton's indiscretions also sparked public debate about sexual ethics in the United States. Some observers lament that Americans have largely abandoned conventional sexual values that discourage casual sex, premarital sex, promiscuity, and adultery. Leon Kass, a professor at the University of Chicago, maintains that the sexual revolution of the 1960s precipitated this decline in traditional sexual ethics. Central to the 1960s ideal of sexual liberation, Kass asserts, was the concept of separating sex from procreation, manifested in society's endorsement of nonmarital sex and contraception. Numerous social changes ensued, Kass argues, including "the destigmatization of bastardy, divorce, infidelity and abortion; the general erosion of shame and awe regarding sexual matters . . . ; [and] the explosive increase in the numbers of young people whose parents have been divorced." In his opinion, the increase in divorce is especially damaging because it has made young people wary of committed relationships and family life.

Katha Pollitt, a columnist for the *Nation*, agrees that American culture has lost its awe about sexuality and that people often find it difficult to establish intimate relationships. However, she does not advocate a return to the days before the sexual revolution: "It was all those shotgun weddings of the 1950s that resulted in the divorces of the sixties. Things loosened up a little, and people were able to get out of bad marriages." Others contend that in spite of the sexual revolution, most Americans continue to disdain promiscuity and infidelity. According to a 1998 NBC News poll, 90 percent of adults believe that adultery is wrong—a finding that mirrors results from opinion surveys of the 1970s and 1980s. Several studies have found, moreover, that teenagers are becoming less inclined to engage in premarital sex. In 1989, the Centers for Disease Control reported that 59 percent of high school students had had sex; in 1994, a Roper Organization study found that only 36 percent of students had had sex. Experts attribute this percentage drop to fear of AIDS, improved sex education, and a moderately conservative moral climate.

The authors of the following chapter offer further examination of America's stance on sexual ethics.

"Our problems of epidemic illegitimacy, divorce, adultery, sexually transmitted diseases, and abortion are byproducts of a Kinsey culture."

Alfred Kinsey's Research Has Undermined Sexual Morality

Teresa R. Wagner

The legacy of sex researcher Alfred C. Kinsey has led to a decline in sexual morality, argues Teresa R. Wagner in the following viewpoint. In Wagner's opinion, Kinsey was a pseudo-scientist who wrongly claimed that a majority of Americans engage in premarital and extramarital sex. Moreover, the author contends, Kinsey espoused the belief that many atypical and deviant sexual behaviors are commonplace and normal. The cultural elite's acceptance of Kinsey's fraudulent claims has undermined traditional sexual ethics and promoted sexual immorality. Wagner is an analyst on human rights and life issues for the Family Research Council, an organization that advocates traditional family values.

As you read, consider the following questions:

1. According to Wagner, from whom did Kinsey receive much of his research data?
2. In the author's opinion, why did much of the American public accept Kinsey's research findings?
3. Which organizations constitute part of the "Kinseyite establishment," in Wagner's view?

Reprinted, with permission, from "From Kinsey to Clinton," by Teresa R. Wagner, from the Family Research Council website, www.frc.org; ©1999 Family Research Council, Washington, D.C.

It is all too fitting that we should have Bill Clinton as our president at the close of the twentieth century. Cultural elites of this era have been devoted to dismantling traditional sexual ethics. Who better to represent this effort than the man who disgraced his presidency and scandalized his country for the sake of sexual immorality and its concealment?

What started with Alfred C. Kinsey has led to Bill Clinton.

On November 6, 1998, approximately 200 people gathered at San Francisco State University to honor Kinsey, the infamous "sex researcher" whose startling work *Sexuality in the Human Male* was published 50 years ago. Author Judith Reisman knows this Kinsey crowd well. This socialist-bred grandmother has spent much of the last 20 years examining the seeds of our sex-saturated culture.

It all started when her 10-year-old daughter was raped by a neighborhood kid. Angry and distraught, Reisman turned to family members around the country for support, only to be told that her daughter might have invited the violation. "Children, you know, are sexual from birth," she was advised.

Reisman's profound need to understand this most callous and insulting response ultimately led her to the Kinsey Institute in Bloomington, Indiana. What she found there was both shocking and revolting, and her book, *Kinsey: Crimes and Consequences*, makes it clear that she wants the world to know.

The Truth About Alfred Kinsey

To many, Alfred C. Kinsey was the quintessential scientist, having spent years studying gall wasps at a staid and conservative midwestern university. Beneath the scholarly veneer, however, was a man virtually obsessed with sex, starting with indulgence of his own homosexual urges and, according to biographer James Jones, leading to practices of sado-masochistic self-stimulation that resulted in a life-threatening infection. As Jones has remarked, these are signs of a "very desperate" man.

Reisman's exposé of Kinsey's life and work focuses first on the fraudulence of his presumably scientific findings. Holding up what looked like reams of data, he told the American public that as many as 85 percent of men and women engaged regularly in both pre- and extramarital sexual relations (of normal and decidedly abnormal kinds). He also claimed that children could and should enjoy sexual activity, since he had "evidence" that they were sexual from birth.

In 1948, when traditional sexual morality was still held up as the standard, these "findings" shocked the nation.

Kinsey never revealed that much of his "data" came from men in prison, convicted of sex crimes as well as other deviant offenses. The "research," carried out mostly from 1941 to 1945, did not reach most American men, who were fighting the war against Hitler.

The pool for women was similarly limited and skewed—mostly prostitutes, strippers, inmates, or some combination of the three. As Reisman notes, no married women or mothers were included.

But Reisman uncovered more than fraud. Beyond the scientific deception are crimes of the worst kind: Kinsey knew about and, arguably, encouraged criminal acts of child molestation.

A 1998 British documentary titled "Secret History: Kinsey's Paedophiles" details the collaboration between Kinsey and at least two known pedophiles, Rex King in the United States and Fritz von Ballusek in Germany. Von Ballusek was an SS officer who would later be arraigned on charges of murdering one of the children he had molested. He was ultimately convicted of sexual assault. According to the legal transcript, von Ballusek said that Kinsey asked him to complete and submit questionnaires about his activities.

The documentary reports that King sexually abused hundreds of children and provided Kinsey with detailed diaries of the encounters. Kinsey wrote the following in a letter to King: "I congratulate you on the research spirit which has led you to collect data over these many years. Everything you've accumulated must find its way into scientific channels." The correspondence and collaboration between them lasted three years.

The documentary also features an Indiana woman whose father and grandfather sexually abused her for years, until she began menstruating. In the film, she recalls the Kinsey questionnaires on "orgasm" that her father regularly sent off in the mail.

At the very least, Kinsey acted as an accessory to these heinous criminal offenses against small children.

Outrageous Claims About Human Sexuality

Despite the discernible fraud and criminality of this "research," the monied and prestigious Rockefeller Foundation not only funded Kinsey's book, but also backed a savvy and unprecedented media campaign preceding its release. This orchestrated hype, documented by Reisman, produced a splash that older Americans vividly remember. It was in this frenzy of sensational publicity that Kinsey's false and outrageous claims about human sexuality first appeared.

Still, that people just accepted Kinsey's assertions as true, when those assertions conflicted with what they knew about themselves and presumably at least minimally about others, is disturbing. But it is hardly mysterious. Aggressive media campaigns to this day deceive Americans into believing the opposite of what they see and experience.

What's more, Americans deeply respect science, seen correctly as the source of advances in critical areas such as medicine and computer technology. If Kinsey had what looked like science on his side, then he could have America on his side, too. Then there were the secular elites of our country, ever intent on ridding America of its Judeo-Christian traditions, especially in matters of sex. For them, Kinsey proved an irresistible icon. His promoters simply tapped into the country's ready modernist mentality, and America was duped.

Fraud and criminality of this kind are upsetting enough. But the Kinsey legacy that we are living today is even worse. Our problems of epidemic illegitimacy, divorce, adultery, sexually transmitted diseases, and abortion are byproducts of a Kinsey culture where sexual impulses of any kind are readily indulged as a matter of health ("outlets" in Kinsey-speak) and legal "right."

We also now suffer a well-financed Kinseyite educational and governmental establishment. This includes SIECUS (Sexual Information and Education Council of the United States), as well as Planned Parenthood and its research arm, the Alan Guttmacher Institute. These entities mask their sex-on-demand advocacy behind pseudo-scientific credentials to promote extramarital sex and government-funded contraception worldwide. All this has developed as outgrowth of the Kinsey fraud and the sexual revolution he helped to launch in our culture.

Normalizing the Abnormal

Much more could be said about the crimes and consequences of Kinsey and his colleague. The main story, however, lies in Kinsey's dishonest efforts to normalize deviance—a concept that brings us back to our current situation.

Defenders of the president, for instance, would have us believe that adultery is no big deal (it's "just" private, consensual sex, and besides, *everybody's doing it and lying about it*). One Clinton fan, in a conversation with this author, perfectly summed up the tendency to normalize deviance: "Deep down," she explained, "we're all perverts."

This claim is senseless on its face. If we were all perverts, the very concept of *perversion* wouldn't exist. This woman's definition would render the term meaningless by normalizing the abnormal.

Kinsey's Outrageous Claims

The most far-reaching [claim of Alfred Kinsey's] is that children naturally are given to initiating sexual acts and that virtually all forms of sexual behavior should be acknowledged as normal and tolerated. Kinsey's verbose prose is hardly quotable but nonetheless radical in its implications. Consider his condescending dismissal of sex between humans and animals: "There is probably no type of human sexual behavior which has been more severely condemned by that segment of the population which happens not to have had such experience, and which accepts the age-old judgment that animal intercourse must evidence a mental abnormality, as well as immorality." Translation: It's all good.

Beverly R. Newman, *Insight*, March 30, 1998.

Her statement, of course, would have made Kinsey proud, since it was his intention to normalize and thereby legitimize behaviors that traditional mores had generally considered "perverse." That is also the goal of much of today's left, with its promotion of sexual license and all that comes with it (funding and promoting the giving of contraceptives to minors, even behind parents' backs; advocating abortion, even during the delivery of a child; and the homosexual rights movement).

Such efforts to chip away at the traditional sexual ethic are the reason that we are so often told that *most* families are dysfunctional, or *most* minor girls are mature enough to get abortions, or *most* of us experience bisexual urges, and so on. The underlying argument is that what has traditionally been regarded as "deviant" is actually "normal," so there is no yardstick left by which to judge.

We should know better. The traditional ethic spared our nation many destabilizing effects, to say nothing of broken hearts and broken lives, however imperfectly it was observed. It did not and does not view sex as merely a sport or a legal "right." It considers human sexuality a great and powerful gift that can be given to another in sign and seal of the love proclaimed in marriage. Once, this was not just an ideal, it was a *norm*. It was beset by human deficiencies to be sure, but it was and is still a standard that offers an alternative to the grim Kinsey destination, where some in our culture would lead us.

Therefore, we need not so much a call to "go back" as a call to look ahead. We can continue down the Kinsey path and end up as unhealthy and unhappy as he was. Or, we can visit the question of human sexuality anew, to learn its rightful place in serving human happiness and dignity.

"A productive debate [on sexual morality] only can flourish in a climate of honesty and respect for varying opinions."

Alfred Kinsey's Research Has Advanced the Study of Human Sexuality

John Bancroft

Several advocacy organizations have denounced researcher Alfred Kinsey and Indiana University's Kinsey Institute for promoting sexual immorality and legitimizing aberrant sexual behavior. In the following viewpoint, John Bancroft argues that Kinsey and his legacy have been wrongly maligned. Kinsey deserves some criticism, Bancroft points out; however, he is an important pioneer in behavioral research whose work has fostered a fuller understanding of human sexuality. The Kinsey Institute, moreover, currently conducts scientific research on topics that policymakers should learn more about in a nation rife with sex-related problems. Bancroft is the director of the Kinsey Institute for Research in Sex, Gender, and Reproduction in Bloomington, Indiana.

As you read, consider the following questions:

1. What allegations constitute part of the "campaign of misinformation" against Alfred Kinsey, according to the author?
2. According to Bancroft, what topic did Kinsey focus on in his final book?

The United States leads the industrialized world in a number of important ways, but they are not all positive. Our country heads the league tables for sex-related problems—teenage pregnancies, sexually transmitted diseases and sexual assaults. We have our fair share of other problems as well, such as child sexual abuse and the common sexual dysfunctions that can undermine the stability of marriage. Yet, we remain ignorant or uncertain about many aspects of these problems. If scientists and policymakers are to tackle them effectively, they must better understand the problems.

Human sexuality is complex; sociocultural and biological determinants must be taken into account. For that reason, we need an ongoing tradition of interdisciplinary scholarship. The Kinsey Institute for Research in Sex, Gender and Reproduction, one of Indiana University's several research institutes, is unique not only in the United States but in the world in its established commitment to such interdisciplinary scholarship.

The Denigration of Alfred Kinsey

So why am I asked to defend state funding of the Kinsey Institute? Because there is an ongoing campaign by vocal and well-funded elements to close it down. Their principal target appears to be sex education. They misguidedly believe that by discrediting Alfred Kinsey, who died more than 40 years ago, they will undermine modern sex education. And what better way to discredit Kinsey than closing down the institute named for him?

In December 1995, the Family Research Council successfully lobbied to introduce a bill into Congress aimed at the institute's federal funding, but that House bill got nowhere. In January 1998, a resolution was passed by the Indiana House of Representatives urging the withdrawal of state funding for the Kinsey Institute; that effort was instigated by Concerned Women for America, or CWA. That measure also died quietly when the Legislature ended its session in February. Both efforts were anchored in a dislike of Kinsey and what he represented—as well as a considerable amount of misinformation.

I recently met with the sponsor of the Indiana resolution,

and discovered that his case was based largely on the current campaign of misinformation from CWA. He had read nothing written by Kinsey himself; he knew nothing about the Kinsey Institute's work and mission today and apparently was not interested. He wanted its closure as a symbolic denigration of Kinsey by Indiana University.

The campaign of misinformation is extraordinary, with statement upon statement with no basis in fact. For example: According to some allegations, Kinsey believed that "all sex laws should be eliminated including laws against rape"; that "there was no moral difference between one sexual outlet and any other"; that the consequences of such beliefs included a 526 percent increase in the number of rapes in the United States; and that Kinsey's "theories" produced a 560 percent increase in crime, a 300 percent increase in out-of-wedlock births, a 200 percent increase in divorce rates and a 200 percent increase in teen suicides. These allegations, and many others like them, are ridiculous.

Sex education today, we are told in this disingenuous campaign, is based on research Kinsey carried out with sexual criminals. Kinsey studied sexual criminals; the Kinsey Institute published a book on "sexual offenders" in 1965 based on this data, which has nothing to do with sex education. Kinsey reported observations of children's sexual responses made by a few of these sexual criminals; the evidence in the much-cited "Table 34" contains information from one such man. The nature of this information, which was made clear in the book, represents a small proportion of the evidence presented about childhood sexuality, a tiny proportion of his two published books, and it has nothing to do with sex education today or in the past. In fact, sex education today is not based on Kinsey's research in any respect. Insofar as sex education relies on research findings, it uses far more recent and relevant research.

Kinsey's Sex Research

Kinsey's research is discredited, we are told by opponents of the institute, because, having interviewed these sexual criminals, he then did not report them to the police.

At the time of Kinsey's research, virtually all forms of sexual activity outside marriage and several forms of sexual activity within marriage (not including raping one's wife) were illegal. He attached great importance to the confidentiality he guaranteed his subjects, and this was crucial to the success of his whole research endeavor.

Kinsey's mission, his detractors claim, was to undermine sexual morality as we know it. In his last book, the volume on the female, he was principally concerned about the lack of sexual understanding between men and women and how this undermined the stability of marriage. Ironically, considering how Kinsey so often has been accused to the contrary, the book underscores that he saw heterosexual marital sex as the norm. True, Kinsey is not beyond criticism. He made mistakes; with the benefit of 50 years of hindsight, one can say that he was naive in several respects. But he was a pioneer who broke through the social taboos to carry out the first substantial survey of sexual behavior, which remains the largest and richest collection of data on sexual behavior ever collected and is used by researchers today.

The Kinsey Institute

What of the institute named for him? The Kinsey Institute fulfills its mission in a number of ways. It has uniquely rich collections of materials relevant to the understanding of human sexuality and how it has changed over time and across cultures. In addition to its extensive library of books and papers, the institute has major collections of photography, art, films and videos as well as archival papers and manuscripts. As we work to preserve these collections and make them more accessible to scholars, so we find a steady increase in demand for access from the academic community.

The institute organizes interdisciplinary meetings, bringing scholars together from around the world and producing publications from these events. The institute has a research program; we are studying the effects of steroidal contraceptives on the sexuality and well-being of women and the impact of such effects on the acceptability and continuation with these methods. This is research that should have been conducted several decades ago. We are exploring with Family Health International how this research methodology can be adapted to address the same questions in other countries in the developing world, tackling an issue of crucial importance to the effectiveness of family-planning programs worldwide. We are investigating the impact of the menstrual cycle on the sexuality of women.

The Kinsey Group

In the mid-1930s Alfred Kinsey and some other Indiana University faculty members were asked to teach a course on marriage and the family. In preparing for the course, Kinsey discovered that there was little scientific information about the sexual aspects of marriage, so he decided to do his own research. Initially, he administered questionnaires to his students about their sexual experiences. By 1938 he had established a research group at Indiana, and members of the group began the first of their interviews with thousands of Americans about their sexual experiences and behaviors. Kinsey and his colleagues, Wardell Pomeroy, Clyde Martin, and Paul Gebhard, undertook the task of describing the sexual behavior of typical Americans throughout the life span by using a combination of intensive interviews and questionnaires.

Elizabeth Rice Allgeier and Albert Richard Allgeier, *Sexual Interactions: Basic Understandings*, 1998.

In the area of male sexuality, we have a novel research program studying the neuropsychology of male sexual response. This research not only may prove to be considerably relevant to understanding common problems of male sexual dysfunction but also may shed light on why some men persist in taking sexual risks, an issue crucial to the HIV/AIDS epidemic. We are collaborating with colleagues in the medical school to use brain-imaging techniques to investigate central mechanisms involved in the control of sexual response.

We have been fortunate to have two postdoctoral fellows funded by the Social Science Research Council's, or SSRC's new Sexuality Research Fellowship program. Last year, our SSRC fellow, a historian, used the institute's archives to further her study of the history of transsexualism in the United States between 1930 and 1970. In 1998 and 1999, we have a fellow studying the relationship between childhood sexual play and adult sexual adjustment by asking young adults to recall their childhood experiences, as well as describing their sexual development during adolescence and since. This data will be compared with data obtained from Kinsey's original survey, permitting the parallel study of two data sets collected 50 years apart. The Kinsey Institute provides specialized clinical services to men and women who have sexual dysfunctions and women with menstrual-cycle-related problems. This form of clinical care, in which both psychological and physical aspects are given equal importance, is threatened by the current health-care system in the United States. Our clinics, and the training of health professionals associated with them, will help to keep these important clinical skills alive and available.

And finally, the institute is attaching increasing importance to its role as an "information service," provided through our World Wide Web site. I would urge anyone who wants to know more about the Kinsey Institute and its current activities to visit us at *http://www.indiana.edu/~kinsey/*.

The Need for Continuing Research

We are legally restricted in how we can use many of the materials in our collections, and because of this we restrict access to scholars with bona fide research interests. However, we are progressively "coming out of the closet." For the last three years we have provided courses for the local community through the university's continuing-studies and mini-university programs. In October 1997, we had our first major public exhibit of items from our art and photography collections. The six-week-long exhibit, "The Art of Desire: Erotic Treasures From the Kinsey Institute," was held in the fine-arts gallery on the Bloomington campus. This effort celebrated the 50th anniversary of the founding of the institute and was a great success. We give tours for an increasing number of visitors to the institute and, following the recent political interest, we have invited state legislators to visit the institute to learn more about our activities. We are proud of the Kinsey Institute, and we believe its role will grow. In fact, the need for interdisciplinary research of this kind is so great today that, rather than closing us down, comparable institutes should be set up on other campuses around the country. Then there will be a reasonable chance that the need for an established tradition of interdisciplinary scholarship in human sexuality will be met.

As for sex education, the Kinsey Institute is not directly involved, but we recognize its importance. It is not a straightforward issue, however. There is need for vigorous debate as well as careful evaluation of the effects of different policies. And, of course, issues of sexual morality will be central to this debate as, I hope, will evidence derived from sound scientific research. But a productive debate only can flourish in a climate of honesty and respect for varying opinions, none of which are in the forecast of the anti-Kinsey movement.

"People are scared to do it with total strangers, but they'll have casual sex with their friends. Catching a disease is not the first thing on their minds."

Youths Are Sexually Permissive

Part I: Kristina Sauerwein; Part II: Don Feder

The authors of the following two-part viewpoint contend that teenagers and young adults are sexually permissive. In part I, freelance journalist Kristina Sauerwein contends that many young people have grown weary of hearing messages about sexual responsibility. These youths engage in casual sex and put themselves at risk for contracting sexually transmitted diseases. In part II, syndicated columnist Don Feder argues that youths are having premarital sex because American culture—including the media and the educational establishment—inundates them with sexually explicit images and messages.

As you read, consider the following questions:

1. According to Sauerwein, in what various ways do young people define monogamy?
2. According to Constance Pilkington, cited by Sauerwein, what is "hooking up"?
3. What is the difference between lovemaking and copulation, in Don Feder's opinion?

Part I: Reprinted, with permission, from "Modern Love," by Kristina Sauerwein, *Los Angeles Times,* January 29, 1996. Copyright, 1996, Los Angeles Times. *Part II:* Reprinted from "Our Culture's Debasement of Sexuality," by Don Feder, *Conservative Chronicle,* July 29, 1998, by permission of Don Feder and Creators Syndicate.

I

Casual sex. Ever had it?

Someone older than 35 answers either yes or no.

The response from younger people? Puzzled faces. Pause. "No. Yes. Uh, no. Kinda-sorta-maybe-I-don't-know."

Makes perfect sense, sex experts say. Boomers easily define casual sex: one-night stand. Passion. A no-strings-attached lover. But it's trickier for the younger generation, who explored their sexuality during what one psychologist called the "sex contradicting" '80s.

Pop culture praised sex purely for pleasure while doctors injected fear of a new disease called AIDS. A just-do-me attitude struggled against scary safe-sex warnings, such as "Forget a Condom and DIE."

Boomers, outgrowing their wild days that defined the sexual revolution, married and made monogamy hip. Younger adults embraced monogamy—but in their own way.

For some, it mirrors the boomer definition. Others say monogamy includes having sex with a person you're "going" with, even if only for a week. It can also be a romp with a good friend who wants pleasure, not a commitment. Or a one-night stand that allows everything but penetration.

Experts Are Worried

However young people define casual sex, health officials, psychologists and sex therapists say they're worried. Each year, 12 million people catch a sexually transmitted disease (STD), with people younger than 30 accounting for about three-fourths of them. The Centers for Disease Control and Prevention reported in 1995 that HIV, the virus that causes AIDS, is the leading cause of death among people 25 to 44; since the disease has an incubation period of up to 10 years, this indicates that they contracted the disease in their teens and 20s.

Like many people in her age group, 26-year-old Marchella defines casual sex as "the opposite of monogamy." Specifically, "It's when you meet someone, say at a bar, and have sex later. I would never do that. I can't think of any friend who would either. It's like begging for some disease."

Yet when she's not in a relationship and the mood strikes, she'll have sex with one of her best friends, a man she met at college. "We both like [the arrangement]," says the graduate student from Los Angeles. "But I wouldn't say it's casual, because we know each other.

"I mean, someone else might think so—someone who's old-fashioned," she says. "But, I guess, I'd say that I'm not having casual sex because it's not like I'm easy or anything."

Confused Sexual Attitudes

That opinion provokes a groan from Peggy Clarke, president of the American Social Health Assn., a nonprofit STD-prevention group in North Carolina. "Young people think they're not prone to STDs because most don't have sex with someone they just met," she says. "But, often, what they're doing is still [casual] sex even if they don't call it that."

Experts call it "serial monogamy." And, they say, it's increasing, particularly because people in their 20s are tired of the safe-sex messages they've heard for more than a decade. They feel invincible. They've been cautious and now feel entitled to as much sexual fun as their parents had in the '60s and '70s. A handful of young people, with end-of-world jitters, say it's best to live it up now in case everyone dies come the millennium.

These reasons lead to confused sexual attitudes, says Toni Bernay, a clinical psychologist in Beverly Hills. "Young people feel anxious," she says. "There have been incredible changes in the 1990s. For example, look at the fall of communism. Those of us who live in L.A. have also lived through the riot, earthquakes, floods and fires. They want their youth. But they don't know what to expect."

Tess never thought she'd catch an STD from a man who enjoyed—and cried during—a rented video of *Fried Green Tomatoes*. "I thought, 'Gosh, he must be very sensitive and sweet. He'd never hurt anyone,'" recalls Tess, a 29-year-old manicurist in the San Fernando Valley.

And then tiny red bumps sprouted around her genital area. "I thought . . . 'What a jerk,'" Tess remembers. "I knew I got it from him because, before that, I was [celibate] for a long time." Later, an acquaintance casually mentioned this man's quest for partners—men and women—to temporarily satisfy his insatiable sex drive.

A lot of young people are like that, says Phillip Lin, 22. "In college, people seem to be looking for immediate pleasure," he says. "People are scared to do it with total strangers, but they'll have casual sex with friends. Catching a disease is not the first thing on their minds."

"Hooking Up"

Curiosity and concern compelled Constance J. Pilkington, assistant psychology professor at William and Mary College in Williamsburg, Va., to research the sexual attitudes of college students. Her job gives her opportunities to listen to students' sexual escapades.

This is how Pilkington learned about "hooking up."

"It's an agreement between two people not involved in relationships to repeatedly have sex without any commitments," she says, explaining that this usually lasts until one of them enters a relationship. "This is happening all over, and they feel OK with it because they're not having sex with strangers."

Increasing Promiscuity

Americans today are far more promiscuous than in the past. One big reason is that people are initiating sexual intercourse at younger ages, which usually leads to a higher number of partners during their lifetime.

According to a national poll of more than 11,000 high-school-aged youths, 54 percent said they were sexually active, compared with 29 percent in 1970. The proportion of 15-year-olds who have had sex has risen from 4.6 percent in 1970 to 26 percent. And almost one-fifth of the sexually active teens say they have had four or more partners.

Gracie S. Hsu, *World & I*, June 1998.

Many members of this generation began worrying about the consequences of sex before they entered their double digits, Pilkington says. "Sexuality was around them at early ages. They were raised with heightened awareness. But after thinking so much about sexual responsibility, many young people are irritated" because they feel deprived of the sexual freedom their parents had.

Jason Greene, 27, is a little more than irritated. "I'm mad," says the plumber from the Northeast. "It's not fair. I'm fed up with hearing about all the great free sex in the '60s and '70s. Now, I hear people [from that era] tell people my age about abstinence. That seems a little hypocritical. What happened to our fun?"

II

It was probably a hoax. But the announcement that two 18-year-olds planned to lose their virginity on the Internet seemed both in keeping with the times and yet another sign of our culture's debasement of sexuality.

The couple, who called themselves "Diane and Mike," said they would have initial intercourse on Aug. 8, 1998, at 9 p.m. EDT, with a camera broadcasting the event live on their Web site. They described themselves as "typical all-American kids" and honor students from churchgoing families.

They said they wanted to show "the beauty of lovemaking" and to "change repressive sexual attitudes."

Life in the Raw

At this writing, it's questionable whether Diane and Mike ever existed. But, assuming it was just a moneymaking scam, now that the idea is out there, how long will it be before an adventurist duo, armed with psuedo-idealism and sniffing a shot at the *Guinness Book of Records*, comes along?

This viewpoint is addressed to them. The sexually repressed attitudes you say you're combatting, where exactly do they hold sway? In the movies? On television? In our schools (where sex education reigns supreme), at art galleries (with their federally funded smut), with our voyeuristic news media? Where is reticence, or even discretion, on the rise?

One evening in July 1998, the top three stories on the nightly newscast I watched were: 1) the administration's attempt to keep Secret Service agents from testifying about their possible knowledge of Don Juan di Pennsylvania Avenue getting it on with Monica Lewinsky, 2) Marv Albert (the back-biting, cross-dressing sportscaster) being hired to do a show on the Madison Square Garden Network, and 3) some geezer who's suing to force his HMO to pay for Viagra.

If that was too much life in the raw, you could turn on HBO, whose new series, *Sex and the City*, is a worthy addition to its parade of pandering—*Real Sex*, *America Undercover* and *Taxicab Confessions.*

The Warner Brothers Network's *Dawson's Creek* is determined to make ABC's *NYPD Blue* look like Barney. A 15-year-old character in this swamp of adolescent hormones claimed losing her virginity at 12 "made me a better person." Imagine how much her character would have been refined if she "became a woman" at 11 or 10?

Hollywood has no monopoly on prurience. An 18-month survey of the Internet, completed in 1995, found 917,410 sexually explicit pictures, film clips and stories. Much of it was far kinkier than what's available on magazine racks, including pedophilia, sadomasochism and a barnyard cast of thousands.

A Soul-Numbing Casualness About Sex

As a result of this saturation, of those in their 20s, three-quarters of males and half of females first had sex between the ages of 15 and 19.

Jaded, world-weary teenie-boppers are bad enough (a recent *Time* magazine story mentioned two 14-year-olds in Salt Lake City asking a nurse at a teen center how to find the "G-spot"), worse is a culture that encourages a soul-numbing casualness about sex.

Societies that take sex seriously don't have high rates of divorce and out-of-wedlock births, not to mention the pathetic phenomenon of 15-year-old girls with a past.

In this atmosphere, how hard is it to imagine a real Diane and Mike? Like everything else in our culture, it's not a matter of if but when.

So what would you tell them? How would you explain to a pair of bright, churchgoing, all-American kids that intimacy is a crucial aspect of lovemaking, that which differentiates it from copulation?

Making love is a gift two people give each other. That it's an experience for two, and not a spectator sport, is part of the enchantment.

Where is the intimacy at an orgy? How do you share yourself with one person while baring your body and soul to the world? How special can the act be if what you give your lover is simultaneously offered to total strangers?

It's only sex. Only the most serious thing two people can do with their clothes off. Only an act that contains the seeds of creation. Only an experience that consummates love and can bind a couple for a lifetime. Why shouldn't it be performed in the cyberspace equivalent of Macy's store window?

Richard Suhre was "appalled" and "repulsed." Oh, not by the prospect of virginity lost on the Internet. No, Suhre, a retired electrical engineer, told a court in July 1998 that he was disgusted by a display of the Ten Commandments in the Haywood County, N.C., courthouse.

He's suing to force its removal. Some things are just too shocking to be shown in public.

"Rising numbers of teens are saying no to sex."

Youths Are Becoming More Sexually Conservative

Frederica Mathewes-Green

The percentage of teenagers engaging in premarital sex has dropped, notes Frederica Mathewes-Green in the following viewpoint. More and more youths believe that nonmarital sex, promiscuity, and abortion are immoral, she maintains. Mathewes-Green attributes this growing sexual conservatism among the young to a national disillusionment with the ideals of sexual liberation and feminism of the 1960s and 1970s. The increasing influence of religious values may also be affecting young people's views on sexual morality, the author concludes. Mathewes-Green is a syndicated columnist and a commentator for National Public Radio.

As you read, consider the following questions:
1. What trio of ideas has harmed American culture for the past thirty years, in Mathewes-Green's opinion?
2. According to the author, what have been the negative consequences of sexual liberation?
3. According to the CBS poll cited by Mathewes-Green, which age group is most likely to define abortion as murder?

Reprinted, with permission, from "Now for Some Good News," by Frederica Mathewes-Green, *First Things*, August/September 1997.

Ideas don't only have consequences, they have companions. For thirty years a ragtag trio has been running across the cultural landscape, linked like escapees from a chain gang and causing similar havoc: "sexual liberation," "economic independence," and "reproductive choice." Even as the bad news is that these notions rose and flourished together, the good news is that hints of their common fall are becoming discernible.

Take sexual liberation (i.e., promiscuity). As recently as 1989 the Centers for Disease Control found that 59 percent of high schoolers had had sex. In subsequent years, similar CDC studies showed the numbers dropping: 54 percent in 1990, and 43 percent in 1992. In 1994, the Roper Organization released a study done in conjunction with SIECUS (the Sex Information and Education Council of the U.S.), which found that only 36 percent of high schoolers had had sex.

A 23 percent drop in five years is notable, if not amazing. What's happening?

The Fallout from Sexual Liberation

"Sexual liberation" sounded like an excellent idea in the seventies, when contraception was abundant and venereal disease rare. Why should men have all the fun? Why should there be an unfair double standard? Women's sexual desires were as strong as men's, and if they weren't they ought to be. In fact, anything men wanted ought to be what women wanted too; in the fretful and self-contradictory thinking of nascent feminism, men were scum, but their values were objects of envy.

Although hammering men for exploiting women and treating them as sex objects, feminists tacitly adopted the "*Playboy* Philosophy" of sex without commitment as the new standard for female sexuality. But gradually women began to realize it was a bad bargain. If girls give sex in order to get love, while boys give love in order to get sex, dumping free sex on the market inevitably drove the cost of love through the roof. Female bargaining power was demolished. Girls had to fling enormous quantities of sex at boys in desperate attempts to buy the smallest units of love. One teen told a friend of mine: "I slept with Rick last night. Do you think he likes me?"

Though "sexual liberation" is still viewed confusedly as something that helps women own and enjoy their sexual feelings, the negative fallout has been hard to ignore: divorce, disease, abortion, illegitimacy, and multiplying heartbreak. Free sex made women feel free in the sense that you feel free falling from a twelve-story building: exposed, vulnerable, and headed for disaster. Thus the phenomenon of "date rape," which is largely the result of uncertainty over what the current rules are for behaving "like a gentleman."

Anti-Promiscuity Messages Are on the Rise

Not only are church-sponsored abstinence clubs booming, but anti-promiscuity messages are popping up in unexpected places as well, perhaps indicating the mainstreaming of the movement. A popular dating handbook, *The Rules*, advises women to refuse sex, reminding them how painful it is when last night's lover doesn't phone, and what power there is in recovering the word "No." And teens in the "straight edge" movement refuse sex, drugs, and alcohol—while dressing like punks, screaming in hardcore bands, belligerently espousing vegetarianism and animal rights, and having no discernible ties to religion.

While rising numbers of teens are saying no to sex, the most telling evidence against "liberation" comes from the kids who said yes. A survey published in the *American Journal of Preventive Medicine* in 1991 asked sexually experienced inner-city junior and senior high students what they thought was the ideal age to begin having sex: 83 percent suggested ages older than they had been. Twenty-five percent of these sexually experienced kids also said that they believe sex before marriage is wrong. (This point of view has continued to grow in popularity. The UCLA Higher Education Research Institute surveys 250,000 new college freshmen every year. In 1987, 52 percent of the students said that casual sex was acceptable; only 42 percent of the 1996 class agrees.)

In the 1994 Roper survey cited above, 62 percent of sexually experienced girls, and 54 percent of all experienced high schoolers, said they "should have waited." And, most poignant, a study published in a 1990 issue of *Family Planning Perspectives* described a questionnaire distributed to one thousand sexually active girls, asking them to check off which item they wanted more information about. Eighty-four percent checked "how to say no without hurting the other person's feelings."

Women's Attempts for Economic Independence

Of all the problems that can be caused by sexual promiscuity, the hardest to ignore is pregnancy. Unexpected pregnancy can be disruptive in many ways, but the bottom line is money: a new mouth to feed historically required the care of two, a full-time caretaker and a full-time breadwinner. Thus, if sexual promiscuity was to be practically feasible, it required that women be economically self-supporting, just in case children came along. Otherwise, a one-night stand might turn into a lifetime commitment. A lifetime commitment might be what women would prefer, but that would undermine the noble goal of "sexual liberation."

Rather than the interdependence of family life, women were exhorted to grasp the mirage of empowerment through "economic independence." As a result, having a high-paying career became the locus of meaning in life. This marked an ironic reversal at the time. The sixties were characterized by rejection of the "corporate rat race" and the material success and status that implied. Instead, we were going to get back to the land, live simply, wear tie-dyes and munch granola.

The feminism that grew out of the sixties did an about-face on this. By the early seventies, the struggle was to get women into that corporate rat race, which now looked all the more appealing for having been off-limits. If men wanted to spend their lives at ulcer-churning work, never seeing their kids, and dying early of stress-related disease, it must be what women wanted too. Particularly in those early days of feminism, child-rearing was disparaged as mindless work for drudges; in this, supposedly progressive women adopted the condescending and contemptuous male chauvinist attitude toward housewives, and toward the work women have done nobly for millennia. It was a wholesale rejection of women's heritage and an adoption of masculine values—values that were, in fact, not very healthy for men either.

"The two-paycheck family is on the decline," reported the

financial weekly *Barron's* in 1994; "the traditional one-paycheck family is now the fastest-growing household unit." Those leading the charge are the youngest moms, between the ages of twenty and twenty-four. One says, "My mother worked; my husband's mother worked; we want our child to have more parental guidance at home." According to William Mattox of the Family Research Council, these young parents feel they were cheated by parental absence growing up, and 62 percent say they intend to spend more time with their kids than their parents did with them.

While feminists continue to wring their hands over the gender wage gap, the fact is that the gap has shrunk to 2 percent—that is, when corrected for variation in lifestyle choices. Childless men and women between the ages of twenty-seven and thirty-three earn nearly the same amount. But a great many women earn less than men because, putting child-rearing and family life first, they choose to work at less stressful and demanding jobs.

Changing Opinions on Abortion

In a world where women are expected to be sexually available, but also expected to be financially self-supporting, the prevention of childbirth—"reproductive choice"—becomes a necessity. Contraception is a partial solution to this problem, but contraception fails, or participants fail to use it for one reason or another. Thus abortion becomes the necessary third link in the chain of companions.

The first year abortion was available, about three-quarters of a million were done; by 1981, the number had doubled to one and a half million. Invention was the mother of necessity: something that people had always managed without (often by turning to adoption plans or marriage) turned into such a handy solution it became nearly indispensable. At the same time, the availability of abortion took away one of women's classic reasons to turn down casual sex, and even made less urgent her insistence on contraception. ("I'll take a chance this one time; I can always have an abortion.") Thus the availability of abortion contributed to an increased rate of unwed sex, "unplanned" pregnancy, and (coming full circle) subsequent abortion. It also made it easier for career to be moved to the top of a woman's agenda, since the distraction of children could so easily be eliminated; indeed, it seemed that abortion was the course a responsible career woman was expected to take, while bearing an unexpected child was unprofessionally whimsical and selfish.

In recent years, the number of abortions has dropped slightly, and public acceptance of the procedure has dimmed. An August 1996 Harris poll found that public support for *Roe v. Wade* had slipped to 52 percent, the lowest point in a decade. The pro-choice movement had dropped nine approval points since 1992, while the pro-life movement had risen five. Polls by CBS News/*New York Times* can be compared as well: in 1989, 40 percent of respondents agreed that "abortion is the same thing as murdering a child." In 1995, that figure had risen to 46 percent.

But that's not the most startling element to the story. In the later CBS poll, one particular age group emerged as the most likely to call abortion murder; they raised the average ten points, to 56 percent. The age group wasn't pious behind-the-times grannies. It was young adults, ages eighteen to twenty-nine.

Many Youths Feel Abortion Is Wrong

At the time of this writing, *Roe v. Wade* is twenty-four years old, which means that every person in America under the age of twenty-four could have been aborted. Of course, a great many were; the ratio has hovered around two or three births to each abortion, and over those years some thirty-five million children were lost. High school and college students can imagine every third or fourth classroom chair reserved for the ghost of an aborted would-be friend or sibling. They know themselves to exist only due to their parents' choice, not due to any inherent value or dignity of their own. Thoughts like these can radicalize.

A study in the April 1992 *Family Planning Perspectives* stumbled over a tendency of teens to oppose abortion. Authors Rebecca Stone and Cynthia Waszak were dismayed to find that the "vast majority" of adolescents in focus-group studies were united in believing abortion to be medically dangerous, emotionally traumatic, and wrong. This finding transcended ethnicity, income level, and gender. Indeed, the young women were even more "judgmental of other women's motives" than the young men, with some opposing abortion even in the case of rape, or alleging that a rape exception would induce some women to lie.

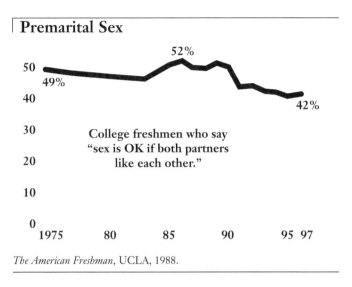

Premarital Sex

College freshmen who say "sex is OK if both partners like each other."

The American Freshman, UCLA, 1988.

Contraceptive failure was not seen as justification for abortion, since the possibility of conception came with the choice of having sex. Abortion was called "selfish" and "a cop-out," and associated consistently with words like "murder," "blood," and "death." The authors attribute this to successful propagandizing by an "intensive antiabortion campaign" (implausibly implying that these kids haven't had sufficient exposure to the arguments for "choice"). Participants believed that life begins at conception, and the right solution to an unexpected pregnancy was having the baby: "Anything's better than killing it," one said.

While reading this study one can almost hear the authors wringing their hands. Though they certainly intended to listen, not lead, in the focus groups, glimpses of ideology struggling against professional restraint slip through. One young woman reminds the group of something the author/facilitator had said earlier: "Religion is legal; we have our choice. Abortion is legal; they have their choice." Perhaps under the influence of such encouragement, most of the adolescents do affirm legal access to abortion (while presuming erroneously that it is presently illegal nearly everywhere, and under nearly all circumstances). In this they reflect the prevalent American compromise: abortion is wrong, but it should be legal. What distresses the authors is the fervency and obstinacy with which the teens think it is wrong; this may "guide their votes later." (Indeed, the UCLA study of college freshmen found that in 1990 65 percent believed abortion should remain legal, but by 1996 only 56 percent agreed.)

A Return to Balance

For all three of these links in a chain of consequential ideas—promiscuity, careerism, and abortion—an inevitable return to balance and health is beginning to occur. In all three cases, the way is being led by teens and young adults, the most encouraging sign of all. What is eliciting such a change is a matter of speculation; perhaps it's the undeniable evidence of past failure, the dawning of reality, a deeper understanding of what really satisfies in life, or a renewed respect for the guidelines offered by biology.

Or maybe it's something else. The authors of the study cited above blamed "antiabortion views, conservative morality, and religion" for forming the teens' attitudes, and throughout the discussions religion did keep rearing its threatening head. The authors report, in a mix of head-scratching bewilderment and dread: "Many of the participants described having personal relationships with God, and some quoted Scripture and said God was the only source of the right advice." The following conversation is quoted:

"A male participant said, 'At the end, legal or illegal, at the end you are gonna pay consequences. Not to man but to God. 'Cause the Bible warns you of what's gonna happen.'

"A young woman added, 'Judgment Day.'

"The young man replied, 'Exactly.'"

> *"The American liberal sees sex in just the way that has led to the current confusion: as a force that must be 'liberated.'"*

Sexual Liberation Has Harmed America

Roger Scruton

Roger Scruton, a writer living in England, is the author of *The Intelligent Person's Guide to Philosophy*. In the following viewpoint, Scruton contends that the scandal surrounding President Bill Clinton's infidelity is one of the latest results of America's sexual revolution—a 1960s movement that emphasized the liberation of sexual desire. Such focus on selfish sexual gratification, the author argues, has damaged American culture by neglecting the importance of chastity, lasting commitments, respect, and trust.

As you read, consider the following questions:
1. What is the "Kinsey view of sex," in Scruton's opinion?
2. According to the author, what was the first result of America's sexual revolution?
3. In Scruton's view, what is the new kind of guilt that Americans face as a result of the sexual revolution?

Reprinted, with permission, from "The Sex Files," by Roger Scruton, *National Review*, October 12, 1998. Copyright ©1998 by National Review, Inc., www.nationalreview.com.

To an outside observer, nothing is more striking in the scandal surrounding President Bill Clinton than the fact that everyone involved is completely bewildered by sex. Indeed, we can see in this humiliating episode the cost that America has paid for the sexual revolution. We in Europe did not escape this revolution; but we did not make it the basis of our lives. Nor did most of us adopt, as so many Americans have adopted, the Kinsey view of sex, as a tingling of the genitals, with orgasm as the goal and the partner as the means to it.

Nor did we draw, as official opinion in America has drawn, the inevitable conclusions of Kinseyism: for example, that there is no difference in principle between heterosexual and homosexual intercourse, that there is no distinction between pure and perverted desire, that chastity is an available choice but not a virtue, and that the only moral questions that surround the sexual act are questions of consent and safety.

But if you draw those conclusions—and the public culture of America, being shaped by the liberal consensus, tends inevitably in this direction—then you cannot condemn the President for what he did; you can condemn him only for the lies that he told about it later.

If, on the other hand, you don't draw those liberal conclusions, you will probably judge the President more harshly. But then you will also be pretty harsh toward Monica Lewinsky, the willing partner in his adultery, and harsh toward Linda Tripp, who taped confidential words about the most intimate details. You would be appalled too by the American media, and by a Congress that has decided to release videotapes of the President's testimony to be broadcast to the eager eyes and ears of the nation's children. You would be amazed that the President has been blamed for evading questions so insolent that no court of law should even consider asking them. And you will, for the thousandth time, recognize what America has lost through the sexual revolution—namely, its innocence.

Results of the Sexual Revolution

The first result of the sexual revolution was not to change people's behavior but to change their conception of sex. Following their "liberation" people no longer made love: they had sex. Having sex does not involve any emotional tie or long-term commitment. It involves nothing more than pleasurable sensations, mutually induced. Once you see sex in this way, the moral landscape changes. The man who has 365 partners a year, all of them strangers, is not for that reason more wicked than the man who confines his attentions to his wife, whom he loves. For, in liberated eyes, they are doing the same thing. If there is a relevant moral question it is that of consent—though why it is so much worse to have sex with an unwilling victim than it is to tickle her, no advocate of sexual liberation has ever explained.

The second result of the sexual revolution was to undermine feminine defenses. If sex is nothing but a tingling of the genitals, why all the fuss? Why the shame and modesty and hesitation? This was Dr. Kinsey's sinister message, and it was greedily lapped up by men, not so greedily by women, who were, however, shamed at last into being shameless. As a result the barrier between the sexes became permeable: the shield which should be breached by love was eaten away by curiosity. Women are now expected to behave like bathhouse homosexuals. However, when women, encouraged to behave in this way, wake up to what they have done, they often experience that peculiar retrospective withdrawal of consent which inspired the new species of female litigation.

This depressing series of events—called "date rape" by the feminists—is taken as further proof of the exploitative nature of men. It is no such thing. It is a proof of the destructiveness of sexual liberation, which has jeopardized everything that gives a woman confidence in her sexual feelings: love, commitment, marriage, and the family. The fury of the American feminist conveys the heartbroken recognition that those things are no longer available except on temporary loan to the very attractive.

A third result of the sexual revolution, and one which is displayed in the personality of Mr. Clinton, is the dwindling of erotic sentiment. That intense concentration on the object of desire, that mysterious longing to possess what cannot be possessed but only cherished, is rapidly going from the world. In place of it has come a simian lust. The focus has shifted from the particular to the general, from the human gaze to the animal function, from the immortal soul to the mortal envelope. The sexual partner is no longer the object of sexual feeling but the means to it—a component in the pleasure machine. We find this view of sex in those who wrote the Ken Starr report, those who gave evidence for it, those who are condemned by it, and those who believe they have the right and need to peruse it.

The Destructiveness of Sexual Liberation

There is no going back on the sexual revolution. But, as ordinary decent Americans have always known, there is no living with it either. The saddest thing, to the outside observer, is the seeming inability of American liberals to oppose the source of decay—which is the view of sex that has held them in thrall. Whether a Kinseyite or Freudian, whether a disciple of Marcuse or a follower of Erich Fromm, whether steeped in the counterculture of the Sixties or newly recruited to the cause of gay liberation, the American liberal sees sex in just the way that has led to the current confusion: as a force that must be "liberated," and which harms us when "repressed." By seeing sex in that way, the liberal changes its nature.

Sexual Lust Must Be Contained

Sex isn't the whole of morality, and moralists' seeming obsession with it often seems disproportionate. Religious conservative leaders do not often declaim in public against the sin of pride, which Christian orthodoxy has generally held to be worse than sexual sin. But the moralists, for all their follies, know something their critics don't: that sexual passion is one of the most powerful and disruptive forces we ever encounter, one capable of inducing irrationality and self-delusion on an epic scale; and that it takes great effort, by individuals and societies, to channel anarchic lusts into civilized patterns of living.

Ramesh Ponnuru, *National Review*, February 8, 1999.

In natural human societies, sex is an existential choice, a source of the deepest desires and the most lasting commitments. The forces which feed our sexual adventures are repressed because they ought to be. Release them from the moral playground and they run wild. And because Americans remain puritans at heart, unable to cultivate the fine art of hypocrisy which pays tribute to virtue in the midst of vice, they have to pretend that this is all okay.

They have to display their sexual insouciance to the world. Hence, throughout American culture—from comic strips to academic journals, from pop songs and chat shows to novels and plays—we find a weird and humorless parody of childish smut. People talk in a deadpan scientistic way about the organs, sensations, and secretions of sex, believing that they free themselves thereby from the mysterious power of erotic feeling. By disenchanting sex they hope to discard their old morality, and the guilt that came with it.

But, as they discover, you do not free yourself from guilt by becoming shameless. You merely open yourself to guilt of another kind. Those who make love secure the loyalty and trust of another person; those who have sex can never be sure that they are so richly rewarded. On the contrary, their sexual adventures are fraught with suspicion. And the cost of this is a new kind of guilt: the guilt of self-betrayal, as the world withdraws its trust, and friendship and respect seem unobtainable.

This is the guilt that stalks America, and which can be seen in the haunted face of Mr. Clinton. It seems hardly fair that he should be expiating a fault that so many of his critics share. But there is a disturbing logic in it too. Clinton's calvary will not redeem America; but it shows the cost of living as though redemption will never be required.

> *"If people could know a lot more about sex in psychological, physiological, sociological ways, they would be more protected against misinformation and hysteria."*

Sexual Misinformation Has Harmed America

Leonore Tiefer, interviewed by Moira Brennan

Americans' knowledge about sexuality has been hampered by misinformation, contends Leonore Tiefer in the following viewpoint. For one thing, she argues, most Americans have an overly narrow understanding of sex, designating it as a purely physical function or as shameful activity. On the other hand, people have been inundated with media images—often unrealistic ones—of sexuality. Conservatives have used the current anxiety created by this overemphasis on sex to rationalize a moratorium on honest public debate about sexual issues, Tiefer maintains. What Americans need is to become better educated about sexuality so that they can put its importance into reasonable perspective, she concludes. Tiefer is a sex therapist and the author of *Sex Is Not a Natural Act*. She is interviewed by Moira Brennan, the copy editor of the feminist magazine *Ms.*

As you read, consider the following questions:

1. What does Tiefer mean by her statement that "sex is fundamentally a cultural phenomenon"?
2. How are ideas about masculinity and femininity affected by Americans' understanding of sexuality, according to the author?

Reprinted from "The Opposite of Sex," an interview of Leonore Tiefer by Moira Brennan, *Ms.*, August/September 1999, by permission of *Ms.* magazine, ©1999.

Moira Brennan: In your book Sex Is Not a Natural Act, *you raise some very provocative questions about our understanding of sex—the very idea of its being "natural," for example. Why are these questions important for feminists?*

Leonore Tiefer: People come at sex with a variety of goals, and sex can be very useful in meeting a lot of different needs. But there is a tendency in this culture to view sex with a very narrow focus—simply as a biological act, or as the domain of the beautiful, or as shameful. I believe that sex is fundamentally a cultural phenomenon. It doesn't exist in a fixed way but is created in relation to whatever is going on in the culture at a given moment.

This is a valuable approach for feminists, because a lot of social issues converge around sex, from reproduction to violence to objectification to disempowerment in intimate situations. It's not about whether someone can achieve orgasm or get an erection, but what are the forces—the social forces, the economic forces—at play? It's rich territory for social criticism as long as we're asking the right questions.

Asking the Right Questions

What do you think are the "right" questions that we should be asking?

One of the problems I think we need to address is what sexuality is. People use the phrase "my sexuality" as though they are only sexual in one way. They say that really comfortably, but I'm not so comfortable with that, because the sexuality that I have with one person is very different than what I have with another person. My experience—I think everybody's experience as they get older—is one of enormous fluctuation in my sexual life. Sexuality is more situational, like friendship. You have the potential for friendship, but it's not like you walk around saying, "Gee, my friendship is really going strong today."

What you put in a category is an important part of how you experience it. When you see the gynecologist, who fiddles with your genitalia, we don't call that sexuality. There's no arousal. There's no orgasm. So what makes something "sexual"? The idea is always to ask, what is this? How does it work in my life? Who says so? Does the way I am looking at it make me happy?

Is there any way we can increase people's understanding of sexuality?

It's the same way as with everything else, through the discussion of real experience. The personal is political. And through much more comprehensive sex education, increasing people's knowledge. If people could know a lot more about sex in psychological, physiological, sociological ways, they would be more protected against misinformation and hysteria. The effects of advertising, for example. We don't teach that in sex ed, and yet it has a profound impact on the sexual experience. And pleasure for the sake of pleasure. Certain commercial interests promote pleasure when it's linked to a product they're selling, but very few people are really trying to bring about an understanding of product-free pleasure. This is an era where Pfizer, the maker of Viagra, is trying to wring every nickel out of every human being on the face of this globe. I want people to be prepared to deal with that.

Nor do I see any members of the clergy writing op-eds or sermons about how we need more comprehensive sex education so that people will be able to better launch into their adult spiritual capabilities, because sex is such a great avenue to spirituality. I recently gave a sermon at my Unitarian Universalist Church called "From Niagara to Viagra: Why Is It So Difficult to Just Talk About Sex?" and my point was that whether it's honeymoon jokes or jokes about Viagra, people can make cracks, but they can't just talk. I started off by saying that I'd been going to this church for 15 years, and I had never heard a single word about sex from the pulpit. I was really glad and really scared to be doing it. But the congregants were wildly enthusiastic. People are parched for this kind of stuff.

A Sexualized Culture

On the other hand, we are inundated by talk of sex in the news, in the movies. That can also feel oppressive.

Well, we live in a sexualized culture as compared to earlier periods of repression and inhibition. The overemphasis on sex by the media is a phase. The behaviors and feelings of people have not changed as much as the commercialization of society, which has exploded. The visibility of sex in the media and its influence on how we understand sex is only 30 or 40 years old. If we were better educated about everything that has changed—the way birth control has shifted the role of sex, the way divorce has done the same thing, the way a good sex life has become synonymous with "success"— maybe we wouldn't feel as oppressed.

Faulty Premises About Sexuality

When we talk about sex to each other, one-on-one, we open a well-worn box of lovers' lies: fake orgasms, promises of fidelity, boastful exploits. But on a social stage, lying about sex grows to such a grandiose level that instead of just answering with fibs and falsehoods, our collective breath doesn't even pose an honest question. The very premises of our education, our media, our aesthetics, assume tremendous beliefs about sexuality that aren't any more real than a flat earth. Instead, double standards and things that go bump in the night are the order of the day, the order of our childhoods, our daily bread.

Susie Bright, *Susie Bright's Sexual State of the Union*, 1997.

All this is complicated by the fact that political conservatives have taken advantage of the anxieties created by this overemphasis on sex. The right, from abstinence education to attacks on *Roe v. Wade*, is very invested in not allowing a discussion about things that they think are morally impure. They believe the mere talking about it is permissive. And there *is* something about the power of secrecy to generate shame and the power of openness to reverse that. So they're right—if we just say words, or allow teachers or books to say certain words, we could be generating the kind of society the right is opposed to: relativistic, morally open, diverse.

We're also inundated with the idea that sex is just biology and can be "fixed" by medicine. That causes a kind of fragmentation in people's thinking. If your focus is on a particular body part as the source of the problem, it prevents you from seeing sex as an act that involves your entire emotional, sensual, intellectual makeup—your whole self. The benefit of bringing a bigger picture to the act of making love is that it can remind you that it's you who is there making love, not some body part that does or does not live up to a medical norm. It's a perspective that honors uniqueness, which is one of the great things we can bring to sex. It's about allowing more humanistic values to be part of the discussion.

Is it hard for people to apply those values to sex?

We don't value our uniqueness in the sexual encounter partly because so much of sex is a secret. You don't see your mother and father making love, but if you did you wouldn't be so inclined to think that you need to look like Michelle Pfeiffer in order to have sex. The cultural messages, whether they are coming from religion or commercialism, are influential in part because they're not counteracted by your own observation. I'm not advocating that everybody watch their parents have sex. But if you stopped to think, you might say to yourself, "I've never seen ordinary people make love. What do they do with a big stomach? How do they undress each other?" I have films of every conceivable kind of person—able-bodied and disabled, fat and thin, old and young—making love, and I can't show them to my medical students because the climate now says any explicit image is pornography and it's degrading. But the lack of this kind of bridge between people's own experience and the culture serves to depress us about sexuality. I think people are depressed constantly about their bodies, attractiveness, and physical expression. It's not so much about what you do with your genitalia that's the problem—it's learning how to feel like a desirable person, and to see that other people are desirable.

Gender Affirmation

Do you think our understanding of sex also affects our understanding of gender?

Gender affirmation is a phenomenally important element in the current construction of sexuality—at least for heterosexuals, who have been the bulk of my clients. Reproduction used to be the essence of gender affirmation for women. And for men it was employment. Now there are fewer and fewer ways of proving gender, and yet it's as important as it ever was. So how do you prove your gender? You've got to be able to have sex—not just any old sex, but coitus. Talking about this in the context of feminism is crucial. It's men's investment in a particular kind of masculinity that is fueling Viagra. Part of the work of feminists has been to question accepted notions about masculinity, whereas you could say Viagra is affirming them.

I worked in the urology department for many years and guys would come in and say, "I'm impotent," and I'd say, "So how is that a problem for you?" And they'd look at me like I was nuts. They'd say, "What? I can't have sex!" And I'd say, "And why do you want to have sex?" in an extremely conversational tone of voice, making eye contact, all of that. And they would say to me, "What do you mean? *Everybody* has sex."

They simply didn't have any answer for these questions. They couldn't answer them because the vocabulary is impoverished, profoundly impoverished. Sometimes somebody would be able to cough up a few words, and they'd say, "It means I'm normal."

Not being able to have an orgasm is like the epitome of not being normal. It's the epitome of not being a man or not being a woman. So I would tell them that there are ways to cope with this. Let's be a man in other ways. No, they couldn't accept that. To them, this was the proof.

I always say to people, orgasm is very American. Because it's a score. It's short. You know when you've had it. You can put the notch on your belt.

How successful have you been when you ask people to reconsider these notions?

It's very hard. I have to admit very modest success. I think my patients would say that I revolutionize their thinking, but from my point of view it's a tiny revolution compared with how I've revolutionized my own thinking. And they don't come for a course on radical sexual thinking. They come to learn how to have an orgasm. I start out by telling them, "Here are 18,000 reasons why it's not as important as you think," but you can't talk somebody out of wanting to have an orgasm. You have to teach them to have an orgasm, and then show them how trivial it really is. It's really a strong neurological twitch, like a convulsion. It's just a reflex. It's the symbolism that makes it feel so good. The symbolism imbues it with dessert and wedding and Nobel prize, all at once.

I try to give people the sense that what's valuable about their sexuality is their story—their own symbolism—rather than how closely they approximate the "healthy norm." People haven't been taught the words for their own stories. There's no vocabulary for anything other than technique. People have a very, very hard time describing the yearnings, the longings, the feelings of gratification surrounding sex.

Sexual Solace

I don't think there's any one way to experience sex. I'm not offering a road map. I say you can use sex in all kinds of ways for any human motive. Solace, nurturance, celebration. And people do. They just don't think of it that way. They look at S/M and they say, "It needs whips and chains, it needs rubber—it's weird." They don't realize that submitting themselves to another person's desire is just one form of pleasure, one that's available to all of us from time to time. Imagine coming home and saying, "This was a really awful day. I don't want to be in charge of myself anymore. You do it. Do me." That sort of subordination could be a welcome relief.

Ritual can work the same way. People go to weddings and things are familiar, they have a certain order and that's comforting. Sex is often ritualized without thinking about it, but I think it can be more intentionally ritualized. You might decide to celebrate the opportunities offered by a sexual encounter the way you'd celebrate the opportunities offered by a Thanksgiving dinner.

During the day, you rarely get an opportunity to express yourself, nobody listens to you, so you get home and you need some affirmation. Sex can do that. The stroking. The relaxing. Approval. When somebody touches you and kisses you and licks you and says you're beautiful, that's approval. The trouble is, for a lot of women it's very hard to accept that somebody thinks they're beautiful. Somebody wants to lick their whole body: what makes a woman feel entitled to that? You've got to feel secure in yourself first.

Do you think part of the reason we don't talk more honestly about sex is because people want to retain some sense of mystery? And is that important?

People have conflicting wishes when it comes to sex.

They want unpredictability and control at the same time. So they tell themselves that if they know too much they will lose the mystery. But in my experience, that's not what happens. I'm an opera lover, and I've seen certain operas a dozen times—I can hum them. Why do I go? All the power and pleasure is still available, even in something you understand well. The idea that the best sex life comes from surrender to the unknown—like in the movies, being swept away by the waves—it's a myth. It's an image. When you talk to people about their sex lives, it's not the surrendering ones who seem to have the best time. Like with everything in life, the more you know about it, the more you enjoy it.

So I want to open up people's minds. Explode those myths. Instead of just talking about an erection or orgasm, let's talk about pleasure. You want pleasure? A lot of pleasure is conditioned. It's anticipation. It's not in the skin. It's not in the genitalia. It's what it means that imbues it with that sense of joy. Otherwise, it's just like eating a peach in the summer. I mean, it's really nice, but it's not ecstatic—well, it depends on the peach, but it's usually not that ecstatic. It's the symbolic investment that makes sex ecstatic.

That's why the best approach is to educate ourselves about the symbolism. Sex is always changing. I don't know exactly what sex used to be like, and I don't know exactly what sex will look like in the year 2150. I don't mind that I don't know. It's not a problem. The idea is to prepare people to deal with the messages they are getting now. I can't stop Pfizer from plowing ahead with Viagra. I can't stop the efforts of the Right. And even if I could, we know from history that something else would pop right up in its place. The point is to educate people to be prepared to deal with these messages in ways that don't infringe on their enjoyment of sex, to keep an open mind and, if possible, to keep a sense of humor about it all.

> *"Cultures have traditionally hedged sex with rules and customs and etiquette, trying to channel its energies and reduce its dangers."*

Misjudgment of the Power of Sexuality Has Harmed America

Peter Steinfels

American culture has deluded itself about sexuality's power, argues Peter Steinfels in the following viewpoint. Traditionally, practices such as marriage enabled society to safely contain and direct the sex drive in healthy ways. Currently, however, established sexual norms are challenged by a modern world that wishes to separate sexuality from reproduction and family life. In effect, the author maintains, sex has become associated with the simple pursuit of pleasure, and its significance as a powerful instinctual drive has been minimized or ignored. The result is a society that is greatly confused about sexuality and sexual ethics. Steinfels is the senior religion correspondent for the *New York Times*.

As you read, consider the following questions:
1. Traditional codes of sexual ethics share what two major premises, in Steinfels's opinion?
2. According to the author, which industries are notorious for exploiting sexuality?
3. How has American society responded to President Bill Clinton's sexual transgressions, according to Steinfels?

M ost traditional codes of sexual ethics, whether set down in sacred texts like the Bible or the Koran, or simply prescribed by tribal customs, share two premises, amply confirmed by recent events: Sex is crazy, and sex is a big deal.

Actually, almost no one really doubts these things, which contemporary culture endlessly celebrates or laments in poetry, song and dance, explores in drama and fiction and even depicts in sculpture and painting.

But at critical junctures, contemporary culture prefers to minimize what it otherwise knows is true. Over the long run, that denial may constitute a more consequential deception than the ones preoccupying the news media and the public. The truth, recorded in folk tales and sacred narratives and epic poems, is that sex wields the power to drive people wild. Indeed, that is one of its chief delights. The man or woman who approaches sex with utter calculation and composure is generally considered repulsive if not immoral.

And sex, the traditional ethical codes and contemporary culture agree, is not only powerful, it is important. It puts the self at stake in a way that even death-defying activities like mountain climbing do not.

Why else do people intuitively take betraying a spouse so seriously, and understand, even while reproving, why someone would lie about it? Why do they automatically put it in a different category than, say, deceiving a spouse about the family budget, although the latter might have no less grave consequences?

Codes of Sexual Ethics

Because of these realities, for which there are plenty of evolutionary explanations, religions and cultures have traditionally hedged sex with rules and customs and etiquette, trying to channel its energies and reduce its dangers.

The young and the single have been coached and compelled to follow certain models and patterns rather than being left to invent their sexual ethics for themselves. Marriage, entry into it and exit from it and everything between, has been ritualized and enclosed in a skein of duties and obligations. The gods and governments have enforced the rules. More immediately, so has the family. Sex, therefore, was both public and private, social and intimate.

Of course, these models and patterns varied widely by faith and from society to society—so that what one group considered normal another might find bizarre or even outrageous. Yet virtually all these codes of sexual ethics assumed two further premises: first, that sex was inevitably linked to reproduction and therefore family lineages and, second, that women were subordinate to men. But modern societies have increasingly rejected these latter premises, and that is a major reason, though perhaps not the only one, traditional codes have been under siege.

Challenges to Traditional Premises About Sex

That siege has often taken the form of challenging the other premises, about the power and importance of sex, as well. The culture that entertains adolescents with retail knockoffs of Dionysian rites and bases whole industries on raging hormones also insists that the sex drive will easily yield to sound information and classroom instruction.

The culture that understands how deeply sexuality is implicated in personality and psychological integrity is also a culture where the moralist warning of sexual anarchy can expect to be derided as an obsessed relic of Victorianism.

It is a culture where advertising and entertainment, in their reliance on sex, exploit its power but trivialize its importance: Sex is exciting but also just one more way to relax and socialize, like bowling, or get a few thrills, like sky diving, or round out the well-appointed life style, like vacationing in exotic locales.

These tactical denials of traditional ethics' insistence on the power and importance of sex have become so pervasive that even a conservative like Representative Henry J. Hyde, Republican of Illinois, has used the word "peccadillo" to describe President Bill Clinton's sexual transgressions.

It is the kind of language that only adds to confusion about whether sex is a private or public matter. Instead of replying "both" and attempting to distinguish when and how, the culture hops from one description to the other. At one moment, reserve and reticence are decried as prudery and censorship. At another moment, publicity and censure are decried as prurience and invasion of privacy.

In reacting to President Clinton's sexual misdeeds, the public has shown itself simultaneously traditional and capable of distinctions. If the President's sexual conduct, for most people, remains a big deal, it is not necessarily the biggest deal. If it cannot be neatly viewed as either a strictly private matter or an eminently public one, the public appears to have settled on distinguishable concerns raised by his behavior—personal trustworthiness versus executive ability, for example—that can be reasonably assigned to one category or the other.

Will this reservoir of common sense guide the society through the adjustments and adaptations in traditional codes of sexual ethics that have been underway, in same respects for a century or more, in others for only a few years?

Certainly that process is not made easier by a culture that, regarding the power and importance of sex, speaks out of both sides of its mouth. The most important lies being told about sex are probably not the ones that have emanated from the White House.

Periodical Bibliography

The following articles have been selected to supplement the diverse views presented in this chapter. Addresses are provided for periodicals not indexed in the *Readers' Guide to Periodical Literature*, the *Alternative Press Index*, the *Social Sciences Index*, or the *Index to Legal Periodicals and Books*.

Ethan Bronner	"Study of Sex Experiencing 2nd Revolution," *New York Times*, December 28, 1997.
Richard T. Cooper	"Survey Finds First Decline in Teenage Sex in 20 Years," *Los Angeles Times*, May 2, 1997. Available from Reprints, Times Mirror Square, Los Angeles, CA 90053.
Cynthia Grenier	"Sex Surge in Women's Magazines," *World & I*, April 1999. Available from 3600 New York Ave. NE, Washington, DC 20002.
Mark Gauvreau Judge	"America's Sexual Right Turn," *Insight*, June 2, 1997. Available from 3600 New York Ave. NE, Washington, DC 20002.
Brett Kahr	"The History of Sexuality: From Ancient Polymorphous Perversity to Modern Genital Love," *Journal of Psychohistory*, Spring 1999. Available from 140 Riverside Drive, Ste. 14H, New York, NY 10024.
Mitchell Kalpakgian	"The Sexual Revolution Is Doomed," *New Oxford Review*, February 1999. Available from 1069 Kains Ave., Berkeley, CA 94706.
John O. McGinnis	"Republic of Lies," *National Review*, October 26, 1998.
Nicolaus Mills	"Our Scarlet Letter Complex," *Dissent*, Fall 1998.
Ms.	Section on Adultery, April/May 1999.
Michael Norman	"Getting Serious About Adultery," *New York Times*, July 4, 1998.
Camille Paglia	"Dissenting Sex," *Index on Censorship*, November/December 1998.
Larry R. Petersen and Gregory V. Donnenwerth	"Secularization and the Influence of Religion on Beliefs About Premarital Sex," *Social Forces*, March 1997.
Stephanie A. Sanders and June Machover Reinisch	"Would You Say You 'Had Sex' If . . . ?" *JAMA*, January 20, 1999. Available from Subscriber Services Center, American Medical Association, 515 N. State St., Chicago, IL 60610.

Wendy Shalit	"Clueless," *Wall Street Journal*, May 21, 1999.
Catherine Walsh	"Perspectives," *America*, February 11, 1995.
David Whitman, Paul Glastris, and Brendan I. Koerner	"Was It Good for Us?" *U.S. News & World Report*, May 19, 1997.

CHAPTER 2

What Sexual Behaviors Should Society Promote?

Chapter Preface

According to a 1999 Rutgers University study, fewer Americans are getting married than at any time in U.S. history. Researchers attribute this trend to the increasing number of heterosexual couples who live together as a precursor—or as an alternative—to marriage. Currently, more than half of all first marriages are preceded by *cohabitation*—the term commonly used to describe the status of unmarried sexual partners who share the same household. Many cohabiting couples perceive their living arrangement as a kind of trial marriage that allows them to see if the relationship will last. "If you're thinking about spending a really long time with someone, you should know that you're compatible in all respects," contends college senior Suzanne Mullane. Cornell University sociologist Marin Clarkberg maintains, furthermore, that cohabitation is an understandably popular alternative for young couples facing uncertain economic circumstances: "Living together and pooling resources in the short run may be a smarter strategy than simply living on one's own while waiting to mature into marriage material." Some couples, though, see no need to exchange legal vows. "This is a marriage in heart and spirit," asserts psychotherapist Amy Pine in describing her live-in relationship of fifteen years. "It's just that we didn't need to have it sanctioned by the government."

Many analysts, however, are disturbed by the prevalence of cohabitation. Several recent studies have concluded that cohabitation weakens marriage and family relationships. One often-cited statistic—that cohabiting couples who marry have a 46 percent higher rate of divorce than noncohabitors who marry—puzzles researchers. Some analysts maintain that cohabiting couples are generally less committed to the idea of wedlock and therefore find it relatively easy to leave a troubled marriage. Others argue that cohabiting itself establishes a relationship pattern that emphasizes personal freedom over commitment—a pattern that is hard for couples to unlearn once they are married. Freelance journalist Esther Crain agrees that cohabitation fosters a noncommittal stance toward love relationships: "[Living together] requires no emotional ties at all: no ceremony, no vows—and no promise to work things out when you hit those inevitable tough times." She contends that couples who choose to live together should, at the very least, be engaged first.

Cohabitation is just one of several topics debated in the following chapter, in which authors advocate conflicting sets of sexual values.

"[Virginity] is sexuality dedicated to hope, to the future, to marital love, to children, and to God."

Premarital Virginity Is Beneficial

Sarah E. Hinlicky

People should remain virgins until they are married, argues Sarah E. Hinlicky in the following viewpoint. Premarital sex can lead to disease, unwanted pregnancy, and emotional scars, the author maintains. Those who choose to abstain from sex until marriage, however, demonstrate a mature sense of responsibility that does not cave in to social fad or manipulative persuasion. Moreover, Hinlicky contends, premarital virginity proclaims one's reverence for marital love, fidelity, and family. Hinlicky is a writer living in New York City and an editorial assistant for *First Things*, a monthly journal focusing on religion and public life.

As you read, consider the following questions:
1. What influences have convinced the author to remain a virgin until marriage?
2. What is "gender-war sexuality," according to Hinlicky?
3. In Hinlicky's opinion, what is powerful about virginity?

Reprinted, with permission, from "Subversive Virginity," by Sarah Hinlicky, *First Things*, October 1998.

Okay, I'll admit it: I am twenty-two years old and still a virgin. Not for lack of opportunity, my vanity hastens to add. Had I ever felt unduly burdened by my unfashionable innocence, I could have found someone to attend to the problem. But I never did. Our mainstream culture tells me that some oppressive force must be the cause of my late-in-life virginity, maybe an inordinate fear of men or God or getting caught. Perhaps it's right, since I can pinpoint a number of influences that have persuaded me to remain a virgin. My mother taught me that self-respect requires self-control, and my father taught me to demand the same from men. I'm enough of a country bumpkin to suspect that contraceptives might not be enough to prevent an unwanted pregnancy or disease, and I think that abortion is killing a baby. I buy into all that Christian doctrine of law and promise, which means that the stuffy old commandments are still binding on my conscience. And I'm even naive enough to believe in permanent, exclusive, divinely ordained love between a man and a woman, a love so valuable that it motivates me to keep my legs tightly crossed in the most tempting of situations.

Is Virginity an Aberration?

In spite of all this, I still think of myself as something of a feminist, since virginity has the result of creating respect for and upholding the value of the woman so inclined. But I have discovered that the reigning feminism of today has little use for it. There was a time when I was foolish enough to look for literature among women's publications that might offer support in my very personal decision. (It's all about choice, after all, isn't it?) The dearth of information on virginity might lead one to believe that it's a taboo subject. However, I was fortunate enough to discover a short article on it in that revered tome of feminism, *Our Bodies, Ourselves.* The most recent edition of the book has a more positive attitude than the edition before it, in that it acknowledges virginity as a legitimate choice and not just a by-product of patriarchy. Still, in less than a page, it presumes to cover the whole range of emotion and experience involved in virginity, which, it seems, consists simply in the notion that a woman should wait until she's really ready to express her sexuality. That's all there is to say about it. Apparently, sexual expression takes place only in and after the act of genital intercourse. Anything subtler—like a feminine love of cooking or tendency to cry at the movies or unsuppressable maternal instinct or cultivation of a wardrobe that will turn heads or even a passionate good-night kiss—is deemed an inadequate demonstration of sexual identity. The unspoken message of *Our Bodies, Ourselves* is clear enough: as long as a woman is a virgin, she remains completely asexual.

Surprisingly, this attitude has infiltrated the thinking of many women my age, who should still be new enough in the web of lies called adulthood to know better. One of my most vivid college memories is of a conversation with a good friend about my (to her) bizarre aberration of virginity. She and another pal had been delving into the gruesome specifics of their past sexual encounters. Finally, after some time, my friend suddenly exclaimed to me, "How do you do it?"

A little taken aback, I said, "Do what?"

"You know," she answered, a little reluctant, perhaps, to use the big bad V-word. "You still haven't . . . slept with anybody. How do you do it? Don't you *want* to?"

The question intrigued me, because it was so utterly beside the point. Of course I want to—what a strange question!—but mere wanting is hardly a proper guide for moral conduct. I assured my concerned friend that my libido was still in proper working order, but then I had to come up with a good reason why I had been paying attention to my inhibitions for all these years. I offered the usual reasons—emotional and physical health, religious convictions, "saving myself" till marriage—but nothing convinced her until I said, "I guess I don't know what I'm missing." She was satisfied with that and ended the conversation.

In one sense, sure, I don't know what I'm missing. And it is common enough among those who *do* know what they're missing to go to great lengths to insure that they don't miss it for very long. In another sense, though, I could list a lot of things that I do know I'm missing: hurt, betrayal, anxiety, self-deception, fear, suspicion, anger, confusion, and the horror of having been used. And those are only emotional aspects; there is also disease, unwanted pregnancy, and abortion. As if to prove my case from the other side, my friend suffered a traumatic betrayal within a month or two of our conversation. It turned out that the man involved would gladly sleep with her, but refused to have a "real relationship"—a sad reality she discovered only after the fact.

Gender-War Sexuality

According to received feminist wisdom, sexuality is to be understood through the twin concepts of power and choice. It's not a matter of anything so banally biological as producing children, or even the more elevated notion of creating intimacy and trust. Sometimes it seems like sex isn't even supposed to be fun. The purpose of female sexuality is to assert power over hapless men, for control, revenge, self-centered pleasure, or forcing a commitment. A woman who declines to express herself in sexual activity, then, has fallen prey to a male-dominated society that wishes to prevent women from becoming powerful. By contrast, it is said, a woman who does become sexually active discovers her power over men and exercises it, supposedly to her personal enhancement.

This is an absurd lie. That kind of gender-war sexuality results only in pyrrhic victories. It's a set-up for disaster, especially for women. Men aren't the ones who get pregnant. And who ever heard of a man purchasing a glossy magazine to learn the secret of snagging a wife? Sacrifice and the relinquishing of power are natural to women—ask any mom—and they are also the secret of feminine appeal. The pretense that aggression and power-mongering are the only options for female sexual success has opened the door to predatory men. The imbalance of power becomes greater than ever in a culture of easy access.

Against this system of mutual exploitation stands the more compelling alternative of virginity. It escapes the ruthless cycle of winning and losing because it refuses to play the game. The promiscuous of both sexes will take their cheap shots at one another, disguising infidelity and selfishness as freedom and independence, and blaming the aftermath on one another. But no one can claim control over a virgin. Virginity is not a matter of asserting power in order to manipulate. It is a refusal to exploit or be exploited. That is real, and responsible, power.

The Appeal of Virginity

But there is more to it than mere escape. There is an undeniable appeal in virginity, something that eludes the resentful feminist's contemptuous label of "prude." A virgin woman is an unattainable object of desire, and it is precisely her unattainability that increases her desirability. Feminism has told a lie in defense of its own promiscuity, namely, that there is no sexual power to be found in virginity. On the contrary, virgin sexuality has extraordinary and unusual power. There's no second-guessing a virgin's motives: her strength comes from a source beyond her transitory whims. It is sexuality dedicated to hope, to the future, to marital love, to children, and to God. Her virginity is, at the same time, a statement of her mature independence from men. It allows a woman to become a whole person in her own right, without needing a man either to revolt against or to complete what she lacks. It is very simple, really: no matter how wonderful, charming, handsome, intelligent, thoughtful, rich, or persuasive he is, he simply cannot have her. A virgin is perfectly unpossessable. Of course, there have been some women who have attempted to claim this independence from men by turning in on themselves and opting for lesbian sexuality instead. But this is just another, perhaps deeper, rejection of their femaleness. The sexes rightly define themselves in their otherness. Lesbianism squelches the design of otherness by drowning womanhood in a sea of sameness, and in the process loses any concept of what makes the female feminine. Virginity upholds simply and honestly that which is valuable in and unique to women.

The corollary of power is choice. Again, the feminist assumes that sexually powerful women will be able to choose their own fates. And again, it is a lie. No one can engage in extramarital sex and then control it. Nowhere is this more apparent than in the moral nightmare of our society's breakdown since the sexual revolution. Some time ago I saw on TV the introduction of the groundbreaking new "female condom." A spokeswoman at a press conference celebrating its grand opening declared joyously the new freedom that it gave to women. "Now women have more bargaining power," she said. "If a man says that he refuses to wear a condom, the woman can counter, fine, I will!" I was dumbstruck by her enthusiasm for the dynamics of the new situation. Why on earth would two people harboring so much animosity towards each other contemplate a sexual encounter? What an appealing choice they have been given the freedom to make!

The dark reality, of course, is that it is not free choice at all when women must convince men to love them and must convince themselves that they are more than just "used goods." There are so many young women I have known for whom freely chosen sexual activity means a brief moment of pleasure—if that—followed by the unchosen side effects of paralyzing uncertainty, anger at the man involved, and finally a deep self-hatred that is impenetrable by feminist analysis. So-called sexual freedom is really just proclaiming oneself to be available for free, and therefore without value. To "choose" such freedom is tantamount to saying that one is worth nothing.

Sex Matters

Admittedly, there are some who say that sex isn't anything nearly so serious or important, but just another recreational activity not substantially different from ping-pong. I don't believe it for a second. I learned most meaningfully from another woman the destructive force of sexuality out of control when I myself was under considerable pressure to cave in to a man's sexual demands. I discussed the prospect with this friend, and after some time she finally said to me, "Don't do it. So far in life you've made all the right choices and I've made all the wrong ones. I care enough about you that I don't want to see you end up like me." Naturally, that made up my mind. Sex does matter; it matters a lot; and I can only hope that those who deny it will wake up to their error before they damage themselves even more.

It is appalling that feminism has propagated lies so destructive to women. It has created the illusion that there is no room for self-discovery outside of sexual behavior. Not only is this a grotesque lie, but it is also an utterly *boring* one. Aside from its implied dismissal of all the world's many riches outside the sexual domain, this false concept has placed stultifying limitations on the range of human relationships. We're told that friendships between men and women are just a cover until they leap into the sack together. While romance is a natural and commendable expression of love between women and men, it is simply not the only option. And in our sexually competitive climate, even romantic love barely deserves the title. Virginity among those seeking marital love would go far to improve the latter's solidity and permanence, creating an atmosphere of honesty and discovery *before* the equally necessary and longed-for consummation. Where feminism sees freedom from men by placing body parts at their disposal in a bizarre game of self-deception, virginity recognizes the equally vulnerable though often overlooked state of men's own hearts and seeks a way to love them for real.

It is puzzling and disturbing to me that regnant feminism has never acknowledged the empowering value of virginity. I tend to think that much of the feminist agenda is more invested in the culture of groundless autonomy and sexual Darwinism than it is in genuinely uplifting women. Of course, virginity is a battle against sexual temptation, and popular culture always opts for the easy way out instead of the character-building struggle. The result is superficial women formed by meaningless choices, worthy of stereotype, rather than laudable women of character, worthy of respect.

Perhaps virginity seems a bit cold, even haughty and heartless. But virginity hardly has exclusive claim on those defects, if it has any claim at all. Promiscuity offers a significantly worse fate. I have a very dear friend who, sadly, is more worldly-wise than I am. By libertine feminist standards she ought to be proud of her conquests and ready for more, but frequently she isn't. The most telling insight about the shambles of her heart came to me once in a phone conversation when we were speculating about our futures. Generally they are filled with exotic travel and adventure and PhDs. This time, however, they were not. She admitted to me that what she really wanted was to be living on a farm in rural Connecticut, raising a horde of children and embroidering tea towels. It is a lovely dream, defiantly unambitious and domestic. But her short, failed sexual relationships haven't taken her any closer to her dream and have left her little hope that she'll ever attain it. I must be honest here: virginity hasn't landed me on a farm in rural Connecticut, either. Sexual innocence is not a guarantee against heartbreak. But there is a crucial difference: I haven't lost a part of myself to someone who has subsequently spurned it, rejected it, and perhaps never cared for it at all.

I sincerely hope that virginity will not be a lifetime project for me. Quite the contrary, my subversive commitment to virginity serves as preparation for another commitment, for loving one man completely and exclusively. Admittedly, there is a minor frustration in my love: I haven't met the man yet (at least, not to my knowledge). But hope, which does not disappoint, sustains me.

"[Premarital sexual] abstinence is a fine idea. . . . But 'abstinence-only' is an opinion. And, as today's brides and grooms tell us, a minority opinion at that."

Premarital Sex Can Be Beneficial

Part I: Valerie Gibson; Part II: Eric Zorn

The authors of the following two-part viewpoint maintain that premarital sex is common and can be beneficial. In part I, journalist Valerie Gibson argues that those who advocate premarital celibacy are often women who wish to return to the days of female submissiveness and dependency on men. These women miss out on experiences that can lead to maturity and happiness, she contends. In part II, syndicated columnist Eric Zorn maintains that premarital sex, when handled responsibly, brings about insights and perspectives that are helpful in making decisions about lifelong commitments.

As you read, consider the following questions:

1. Who are the "Waiters," according to Gibson?
2. According to scientific surveys cited by Zorn, what percentage of men and what percentage of women remain virgins until married?
3. In Zorn's opinion, people should wait until about what age to have sex?

Part I: Reprinted from "Intimacies," by Valerie Gibson, *The Toronto Sun*, June 15, 1999, with permission from *The Toronto Sun*. *Part II:* Reprinted from "Save It for Marriage? Most of Us Rewrote That Fact of Life," by Eric Zorn, *Liberal Opinion Week*, July 20, 1998, with permission from Knight Ridder/Tribune Information Services.

I

I guess here's an organization I won't be joining.
Or, to be more honest, can't join.

It's True Love Waits, an organization formed in Nashville, Tenn., that promotes chastity and virginity and eschews premarital sex.

It apparently has hundreds of thousands of members called Waiters who pledge a lifelong commitment to sexual abstinence until they enter what they call "a biblical marriage relationship."

They preach that adherence to premarital celibacy will mean "The Right Partner will materialize and True Love and Holy Matrimony will follow."

Which, to me, is like saying "use this cream and you too will look like Cindy Crawford" and just about as realistic, but everyone is entitled to their fantasies.

The Sexual Modesty Movement

But the high ideals of True Love Waits are just part of a new movement of so-called "sexual modesty" that's being promoted as a "backlash to the sexual revolution and feminism."

Hanging onto virginity is their major platform. It's being touted as "power celibacy" by such virginity gurus as Wendy Shalit, the 23-year-old, self-professed virgin, author of *A Return to Modesty: Discovering the Lost Virtue*.

Shalit states that women haven't made any progress at all with their liberation. She basically says the sexual revolution has been a total failure and women should return to the old style of relationship and way of life. By that she apparently means no sex before marriage, taking his name afterwards, dressing modestly and expecting the man to take care of her.

Ho hum. Shades of *The Rules* (the best-selling books that said the way to get Mr. Right was to go back to a '50s-style of female submissiveness).

As I said, everyone's entitled to their dreams, or foolishness, depending how you look at it.

As Shalit is only 23 years old, I can forgive her naive stance as she obviously has not yet discovered real life—or real men. Or maybe she just hasn't noticed that it's not just women that have changed, but men as well, not to mention our entire modern civilization and way of life.

A Wealth of Choices

Quite frankly, I don't think many men want (or can afford) women to return to being totally dependent on them, despite the perhaps somewhat alluring fantasy of virginal maidens hanging about everywhere waiting for their commands.

But then (perhaps obviously), I've always thought of a continuing state of virginity as an emotional and physical wasteland. I certainly would never consider it to be a bargaining tool in getting what I want from a man.

That may have worked once when that was all the collateral a woman could offer in exchange for marriage and security and there were little or no choices for women beyond the institution. But liberation from marital and financial servitude has given us a wealth of fabulous and far-reaching life choices. What we do with those choices, good or bad, is up to us as educated individuals and has meant we no longer have to submit to society's restrictive dictates in order to survive.

Experience Is Beneficial

In my opinion, a lot of these young proponents of the sexual-modesty movement are simply lazy.

They want to return to the old-style dependent marriage and virginity-as-desirable simply because it's the easy route through life. Let's face it, it's nice and a lot less stressful to have someone else pay for everything, keep you and take care of you. Trouble is that such total dependency doesn't present too many challenges to experience the fullness of life, which helps develop character, experience and knowledge. And they're not just precious assets in a well-developed contemporary woman but an excellent basis for self-preservation if life takes a difficult turn, as it often does.

The other point is that by staying a virgin, you certainly don't have to be bothered with the intricacies of the male psyche, in or out of bed. Standing back all detached and unavailable and waiting to learn it all after marriage can be a disaster. For sure, it doesn't offer the guarantee of lasting marital joy and happiness the modesty folk say it does.

To me, one of the major joys of life is sharing personal and sexual intimacy with men. Okay, so it can be more learning than you need and sometimes a tough experience. But, again, that's how we learn about life and each other.

This whole sexual-modesty gig, far from offering a return to old values, smacks of self-centredness and calculating barter to me, not to say ineffectiveness.

I have a feeling that a few years from now, there are still going to be a lot of these sexual modesty gals about.

Sour and single.

II

Readers of *Bride's* may be an unusually randy bunch, so we must use some caution in approaching the results of the magazine's wedding-night survey publish in its August/September 1998 issue.

Out of 3,000 engaged couples who responded, just 4 percent of the women and 1 percent of the men reported that they will be virgins when they exchange vows. For women, the figure was down from 14 percent in a similar *Bride's* survey in 1988, and on average, the women in 1998 reported having had six other sex partners aside from their husbands-to-be.

Is Sex Sinful?

If one regards sex as sinful in the unmarried state, one is liable to regard it as sinful in the married state. Such an attitude has a melancholy effect on the nurture of the young. Can we have abiding affection for our children when we regard the very act by which they are conceived to be sin-laden? Family values, the clarion call of the nation's hypocrites, are thereby endangered.

William Edelen, *Truth Seeker*, vol. 125, 1998.

More scientific surveys have put the wedding-virginity rate at 7 to 16 percent for men and 20 to 30 percent for women, but either way the numbers suggest two things:

1. The federal guidelines for abstinence-only education—a fad pushed by social and religious conservatives and funded generously by taxpayers—are based on wishful thinking.
2. The "But what did you do, mom and dad?" question

about sex is going to be even more awkward for today's parents than the same question has been about illegal-drug usage.

The guidelines for state programs taking advantage of the $50 million Congress now allocates annually for no-sex education say teachers must tell students that "abstinence from sexual activity outside marriage (is) the expected standard . . . (and) that a mutually faithful monogamous relationship in the context of marriage is the expected standard of human sexual activity."

Pre-Marital Sex Is Standard

In reality, however, pre-marital and non-marital sex are standard practice in this country. An expectation that the man and woman you see standing at the altar or in front of a justice of the peace have never had sex is likely to be crushed by the truth.

Abstinence-only backers respond that "standard" here refers to a moral requirement, not a mathematical result or popularity poll. Pre-marital sex is bad, they say. Or, in the language of the federal guidelines: "Sexual activity outside the context of marriage is likely to have harmful psychological and physical effects."

But what did you do, mom and dad? Surveys say . . . you probably indulged in the deed without the benefit of clergy at least a time or two. And it's my guess you weren't just "experimenting," the No. 1 old drug-use dodge, and you'd be less than candid if you said that you consider it all "a mistake," the No. 2 dodge.

Sexuality Is Complicated

Sometimes it was a mistake, of course. Sexuality is a complicated thing—dynamite in all metaphorical senses. When it explodes in your face, it's often because you misunderstood it, yourself or someone else.

When it doesn't explode, it can take you to new levels of intimacy where you can learn valuable lessons about yourself and gain some of the perspective necessary for wisdom. This comes in handy later when you're pondering lifelong commitments.

Through such relationships you can learn what sex is and what it isn't; who you are and who you are not. Speaking for myself—one who belongs in the mainstream of *Bride's* readership, so to speak—I have regrets about certain indiscretions and related pain both received and inflicted. But overall I consider it to have been a real plus that I did not enter my now 13-year "faithful monogamous relationship in the context of marriage" as a virgin.

The Wisest Choice

What to tell the kids? They can smell hypocrisy at 100 yards, and "just say no" coming from an experienced generation that just said "oh, yes" is not likely to be persuasive, even in an age when sexually transmitted diseases pose a greater threat than in the past.

Yet that very experience also tells what we can say without reservation: Delay, restraint, moderation, contraception, love and respect are key elements of sexual responsibility. Holding off until at least the late teen years is by far the wisest choice.

Abstinence is a fine idea. It was never presented as an option to the students in my schools in the 1970s, and it should have been.

But "abstinence-only" is an opinion. And, as today's brides and grooms tell us, a minority opinion at that.

"Living together helps you see past romanticized notions and clue in to what marriage will really be like."

Couples Should Live Together Before Marriage

Part I: Robyn Brown; Part II: Susan S. Lang

The following two-part viewpoint extols the advantages enjoyed by unmarried sexual partners who live together. In part I, *Glamour* writer Robyn Brown contends that cohabitation is a kind of trial marriage that allows couples to learn about each other's less attractive sides, enabling them to make better-informed decisions about the future of the relationship. In part II, reporter Susan S. Lang discusses the findings of Marin Clarkberg, a Cornell University sociologist who researched the economic circumstances of cohabiting couples. Clarkberg found that cohabitation permits couples with less stable incomes to pool resources while enjoying an intimate relationship that often evolves into a marriage.

As you read, consider the following questions:

1. What does Brown's friend, Rebecca, enjoy about her live-in relationship?
2. According to Clarkberg, as cited by Lang, what percentage of couples who married in the 1990s lived together first?
3. Why do higher-income women cohabit, according to Lang?

Part I: Reprinted, with permission, from "Mock Marriage: Pro," by Robyn Brown, *Cosmopolitan*, September 1, 1998. *Part II:* Reprinted, with permission, from "Money, Jobs Decide Who Cohabits or Marries," by Susan Lang, Cornell News Service, Cornell University, published at www.newswise.com/articles/1999/2/COHABIT.CNS.html.

I

I'm living in sin and loving it. About a year ago, my boyfriend, Tom, and I moved in together. While we suspected that marriage might be in our future, neither of us was chomping at the bit to make me a Mrs. So we decided to try living together. And I've since discovered that in addition to making great financial sense—one apartment is a lot cheaper than two—there are plenty of other reasons cohabitation is nonmarital bliss.

Learning About Your Partner

• *An ideal husband.* You wouldn't buy a car without taking it for a test-drive, and it's no different with a man. Tom and I dated for three years before we shacked up, and I've learned more about him this past year than all the others combined. Living together is like taking a crash course in all of each other's quirks. And let's be honest—do you really want to wait until you're married to find out he goes berserk if he sees a single crumb on the kitchen counter? And doesn't he deserve to know that you have a pathological obsession with *Party of Five*? Believe me, if you're going to share everything, everything matters.

• *Mighty morphin'.* You may know the man you're dating, but you don't necessarily know what he's like to live with. Some men make good boyfriends but lousy husbands. My friend Meredith says that living with her fiance, Scott, for a few months saved her from a marriage that she's certain would have ended in disaster. Meredith says Scott was always a dream date—courteous, sweet, and dripping with class. But after they moved in together, he turned into a Neanderthal. "His half eaten salami sandwiches were in every room, and he absolutely refused to clean up after himself—even after we found bugs in the house," Meredith recalls. "That's when I realized that my husband-to-be wasn't classy, just a spoiled slob." One morning, Meredith poured herself cereal for breakfast and noticed little larvae in the bowl. Her bags were packed by noon.

• *Flash forward.* Living together is like flooring the gas pedal on your relationship—its 24-7 intensity accelerates

84

whatever is going to happen next, for better or for worse. My friend Stephanie, for instance, says that moving in with her longtime lover was the best decision she ever made because it drove her to dump him. "Our so-so relationship would have dragged on indefinitely if we hadn't decided to push it and see," says Stephanie. "Spending all that time together gave me the chance to see the real, nondate him—and the real him was an emotionally distant jerk."

Part of the reason living together shifts your relationship into fourth gear is that it guarantees you'll get a peek at each other's less attractive sides. He'll see you turning in for the night with your face covered in Clearasil. You'll walk in on him lip-synching in the bathroom mirror. Sharing these dirty little secrets can bring the two of you even closer together or send you screaming into the night.

• *The single best reason.* I know, I know. He won't buy the cow if he can have the milk for free. But who decided Bessie was even for sale? My friend Rebecca says that she loves living with her boyfriend, Lionel, and has no intentions of tying the knot anytime in the near future. "I love that our lives are entwined but still separate," Rebecca explains. "Some day in the future I may want to be married, but for now, I'm still really enjoying my singleness."

• *Real romantic.* On the other hand, my friend Alexis never lived with her boyfriend Paul until they had a wedding so expensive it would have made Donald Trump cry. A month later, she called me and told me she was getting a divorce— turns out marriage wasn't anything like she had imagined it. "The first couple weeks were really fun. It was just like playing house," recalls Alexis. "But after a while the novelty wore off, and we started to see marriage for what it really is—a lot of hard work. Whose job is it to balance the checkbook? Should we invest some of our savings in the stock market? Our romantic relationship just was not ready to withstand that kind of strain."

The only thing perfect about marriage is the airbrushed wedding photo. Living together helps you see past romanticized notions and clue in to what marriage will really be like. If my boyfriend and I ever decide to tie the knot, it will mean even more, because we'll both fully understand the vows that we're taking. When they say "Do you promise to love, honor, and cherish," we'll know what they're really asking. Can you be patient when he calls for the third time to say he still hasn't left the office? Do you truly want to be with a man who refuses to eat a single green vegetable? Can you live a lifetime of sleeping with the TV on? Well, if it means I get to wake up every day next to him, I do.

II

Changing values may not be the only reason why an increasing trend across the country is for couples to live together without being married. As with many things in life, money also plays a major role, according to a Cornell University study.

Cohabitation tends to appeal to people in different economic circumstances from those who opt directly for marriage, says Marin Clarkberg, assistant professor of sociology at Cornell, in the March 1999 issue of the scholarly journal *Social Forces*.

On the one hand, she writes, women who choose cohabitation are more likely to earn more than either single or married women, whereas men who cohabit typically earn far less money than men who marry. On the other hand, both men and women who cohabit have less stable job histories than singles or spouses.

Not a Result of Weak Family Values

These findings suggest that cohabitation isn't necessarily driven by weak "family values" and may not always be a "middle" ground between being single and married. Clarkberg asserts that cohabitation attracts people in certain economic circumstances—those, for example, who work in low-stability "McJobs." Surprisingly, Clarkberg says, although economic uncertainty seems to prevent some couples from proceeding down the aisle, it promotes cohabitation.

Clarkberg analyzed data on 12,841 participants in the National Longitudinal Study of the High School Class of 1972, administered in 1972, 1973, 1974, 1976, 1979 and 1986. Although the data set excluded high school dropouts, it was useful for tracking careers, income, earnings and employment experiences.

She says that a little more than half of all couples who married in the 1990s have lived together first. Clarkberg notes that the general trend is that about 60 percent of all couples who live together eventually end up tying the knot.

The Advantages of Cohabitation

Craig Groehn, licensed therapist at the Hope Clinic [in Ames, Iowa], said between 35 to 40 percent of the couples he works with live together before getting married.

"I think many people live together because of fearfulness about making commitments to a relationship they're uncertain about," Groehn said. "[Cohabiting is] how they can maintain independence and at the same time have the advantages of the relationship.". . .

Groehn said the advantage of cohabitation is that people do get to try out the relationship and see how they will manage financial, sexual and emotional issues.

"They also have a chance to disengage if it's not meeting their needs," he said.

Ben Godar, *Iowa State Daily*, October 20, 1998.

Over the past decade, cohabitation has soared by 85 percent, with almost 3.7 million American households now composed of unmarried couples. There are about 75 million households in the United States with more than one person in them.

"Once couples cohabit because of their economic circumstances, the cohabitation may become a slippery slope to marriage. In other words, couples decide to live together for economic reasons and as an expedient way to have a sexual relationship. Once they are cohabiting, though, it brings the question of marriage to the forefront, becoming a pathway to marriage."

A Smarter Strategy

She adds, "For those unsure about their economic prospects, living together and pooling resources in the short run may be a smarter strategy than simply living on one's own while waiting to mature into marriage material."

Then why do higher-earning women cohabit? Clarkberg speculates that these women may opt for living with their boyfriends as a way to enjoy the benefits of couplehood without having to sacrifice their careers during a critical career-building time. Cohabitation might also relieve women of the heavy burden of household responsibilities that wives often take on. Other studies have found that although cohabitating women do far more housework than their live-in boyfriends, they do substantially less than married women.

Clarkberg's study was supported, in part, by the Cornell Employment and Family Careers Institute, a Sloan Center for the Study of Working Families.

> *"Living together before marriage may seem like a harmless or even a progressive family trend until one takes a careful look at the evidence."*

Couples Should Not Live Together Before Marriage

David Popenoe and Barbara Dafoe Whitehead

David Popenoe and Barbara Dafoe Whitehead are codirectors of the National Marriage Project at Rutgers University in New Brunswick, New Jersey. They have each written extensively on marriage and family-related issues. In the following viewpoint, Popenoe and Whitehead argue that cohabitation is having a detrimental effect on marriage in the United States. Cohabiting couples who marry are more likely to divorce than noncohabitors who marry, they point out. The reason for this higher marital failure rate among cohabitors is probably because they are more committed to their personal sense of independence than they are to the continuation of a relationship. Instead of institutionalizing cohabitation, American society should concentrate on revitalizing marriage, the authors conclude.

As you read, consider the following questions:

1. According to the authors, what percentage of high school seniors believe that cohabitation is a good idea?
2. What is especially problematic about serial cohabitation, according to Popenoe and Whitehead?
3. Under what circumstances does cohabitation *not* have a detrimental effect on marriage, according to the authors?

Excerpted from "Should We Live Together? What Young Adults Need to Know About Cohabitation Before Marriage," by David Popenoe and Barbara Dafoe Whitehead, published as part of The National Marriage Project's Next Generation Series, at www.smartmarriages.com/cohabit.html. Reprinted by permission of the authors.

L iving together before marriage is one of America's most significant and unexpected family trends. By simple definition, living together—or unmarried cohabitation—is the status of couples who are sexual partners, not married to each other, and sharing a household. By 1997, the total number of unmarried couples in America topped 4 million, up from less than half a million in 1960. It is estimated that about a quarter of unmarried women between the ages of 25 and 39 are currently living with a partner and about half have lived at some time with an unmarried partner (the data are typically reported for women but not for men). Over half of all first marriages are now preceded by cohabitation, compared to virtually none earlier in the twentieth century.

Widespread Acceptance of Cohabitation

What makes cohabitation so significant is not only its prevalence but also its widespread popular acceptance. In recent representative national surveys nearly 60% of high school seniors indicated that they "agreed" or "mostly agreed" with the statement "it is usually a good idea for a couple to live together before getting married in order to find out whether they really get along." And nearly three quarters of the students, slightly more girls than boys, stated that "a man and a woman who live together without being married" are either "experimenting with a worthwhile alternative lifestyle" or "doing their own thing and not affecting anyone else."

Unlike divorce or unwed childbearing, the trend toward cohabitation has inspired virtually no public comment or criticism. It is hard to believe that across America, only thirty years ago, living together for unmarried, heterosexual couples was against the law. And it was considered immoral—living in sin—or at the very least highly improper. Women who provided sexual and housekeeping services to a man without the benefits of marriage were regarded as fools at best and morally loose at worst. A double standard existed, but cohabiting men were certainly not regarded with approbation.

Today, the old view of cohabitation seems yet another example of the repressive Victorian norms. The new view is that cohabitation represents a more progressive approach to intimate relationships. How much healthier women are to be free of social pressure to marry and stigma when they don't. How much better off people are today to be able to exercise choice in their sexual and domestic arrangements. How much better off marriage can be, and how many divorces can be avoided, when sexual relationships start with a trial period.

Surprisingly, much of the accumulating social science research suggests otherwise. What most cohabiting couples don't know, and what in fact few people know, are the conclusions of many recent studies on unmarried cohabitation and its implications for young people and for society. Living together before marriage may seem like a harmless or even a progressive family trend until one takes a careful look at the evidence.

How Cohabitation May Contribute to Marital Failure

The vast majority of young women today want to marry and have children. And many of these women and most young men see cohabitation as a way to test marital compatibility and improve the chances of long-lasting marriage. Their reasoning is as follows: Given the high levels of divorce, why be in a hurry to marry? Why not test marital compatibility by sharing a bed and a bathroom for a year or even longer? If it doesn't work out, one can simply move out. According to this reasoning, cohabitation weeds out unsuitable partners through a process of natural de-selection. Over time, perhaps after several living-together relationships, a person will eventually find a marriageable mate.

The social science evidence challenges this idea that cohabiting ensures greater marital compatibility and thereby promotes stronger and more enduring marriages. Cohabitation does not reduce the likelihood of eventual divorce; in fact, it may lead to a higher divorce risk. Although the association was stronger a decade or two ago and has diminished in the younger generations, virtually all research on the topic has determined that the chances of divorce ending a marriage preceded by cohabitation are significantly greater than for a marriage not preceded by cohabitation. A 1992 study of 3,300 cases, for example, based on the 1987 National Survey of Families and Households, found that in their marriages prior cohabitors "are estimated to have a hazard of dissolution that is about 46% higher than for non-cohabitors." The authors of this study concluded, after reviewing all previous studies, that the enhanced risk of marital disruption following cohabitation "is beginning to take on the status of an empirical generalization."

Cohabitation Offers Less

The decline in marriage is intimately connected to the rise in cohabitation—living with someone in a sexual relationship without being married. Although Americans are less likely to be wed today than they were several decades ago, if both marriage and cohabitation are counted, they are about as likely to be "coupled." If cohabitation provides the same benefits to individuals marriage does, then is it necessary to be concerned about this shift? Yes, because a valuable social institution arguably is being replaced by one that demands and offers less.

Linda J. Waite, *USA Today*, January 1, 1999.

More in question within the research community is why the striking statistical association between cohabitation and divorce should exist. Perhaps the most obvious explanation is that those people willing to cohabit are more unconventional than others and less committed to the institution of marriage. These are the same people then, who more easily will leave a marriage if it becomes troublesome. By this explanation, cohabitation doesn't cause divorce but is merely associated with it because the same type of people are involved in both phenomena.

There is some empirical support for this position. Yet even when this "selection effect" is carefully controlled statistically a negative effect of cohabitation on later marriage stability still remains. And no positive contribution of cohabitation to marriage has been ever been found.

The reasons for cohabitation's negative effects are not fully understood. One may be that while marriages are held together largely by a strong ethic of commitment, cohabiting relationships by their very nature tend to undercut this ethic. Although cohabiting relationships are like marriages in many ways—shared dwelling, economic union (at least in part), sexual intimacy, often even children—they typically differ in the levels of commitment and autonomy involved. According to recent studies cohabitants tend not to be as committed as married couples in their dedication to the continuation of the relationship and reluctance to terminate it, and they are more oriented toward their own personal autonomy. It is reasonable to speculate, based on these studies, that once this low-commitment, high-autonomy pattern of relating is learned, it becomes hard to unlearn.

Increased Acceptance of Divorce

The results of several studies suggest that cohabitation may change partners' attitudes toward the institution of marriage, contributing to either making marriage less likely, or if marriage takes place, less successful. A 1997 longitudinal study conducted by demographers at Pennsylvania State University concluded, for example, "cohabitation increased young people's acceptance of divorce, but other independent living experiences did not." And "the more months of exposure to cohabitation that young people experienced, the less enthusiastic they were toward marriage and childbearing."

Particularly problematic is serial cohabitation. One study determined that the effect of cohabitation on later marital instability is found only when one or both partners had previously cohabited with someone other than their spouse. A reason for this could be that the experience of dissolving one cohabiting relationship generates a greater willingness to dissolve later relationships. People's tolerance for unhappiness is diminished, and they will scrap a marriage that might otherwise be salvaged. This may be similar to the attitudinal effects of divorce; going through a divorce makes one more tolerant of divorce.

If the conclusions of these studies hold up under further investigation, they may hold the answer to the question of why premarital cohabitation should affect the stability of a later marriage. The act of cohabitation generates changes in people's attitudes toward marriage that make the stability of marriage less likely. Society-wide, therefore, the growth of cohabitation will tend to further weaken marriage as an institution.

An important caveat must be inserted here. There is a growing understanding among researchers that different types and life-patterns of cohabitation must be distinguished clearly from each other. Cohabitation that is an immediate prelude to marriage, or prenuptial cohabitation—both partners plan to marry each other in the near future—is different from cohabitation that is an alternative to marriage. There is some evidence to support the proposition that living together for a short period of time with the person one intends to marry has no adverse effects on the subsequent marriage. Cohabitation in this case appears to be very similar to marriage; it merely takes place during the engagement period. This proposition would appear to be less true, however, when one or both of the partners has had prior experience with cohabitation, or brings children into the relationship.

Cohabitation as an Alternative to Marriage

Most cohabiting relationships are relatively short lived and an estimated 60% end in marriage. Still, a surprising number are essentially alternatives to marriage and that number is increasing. This should be of great national concern, not only for what the growth of cohabitation is doing to the institution of marriage but for what it is doing, or not doing, for the participants involved. In general, cohabiting relationships tend to be less satisfactory than marriage relationships.

Except perhaps for the short-term prenuptial type of cohabitation, and probably also for the post-marriage cohabiting relationships of seniors and retired people who typically cohabit rather than marry for economic reasons, cohabitation and marriage relationships are qualitatively different. Cohabiting couples report lower levels of happiness, lower levels of sexual exclusivity and sexual satisfaction, and poorer relationships with their parents. One reason is that, as several sociologists not surprisingly concluded after a careful analysis, in unmarried cohabitation "levels of certainty about the relationship are lower than in marriage."

It is easy to understand, therefore, why cohabiting is inherently much less stable than marriage and why, especially in view of the fact that it is easier to terminate, the break-up rate of cohabitors is far higher than for married partners. Within two years about half of all cohabiting relationships end in either marriage or a parting of the ways, and after five years only about 10% of couples are still cohabiting (data from the late 1980s). In comparison, only about 45% of first marriages today are expected to break up over the course of a lifetime. . . .

The Need to Revitalize Marriage

Despite its widespread acceptance by the young, the remarkable growth of unmarried cohabitation in recent years does not appear to be in children's or the society's best interest. The evidence suggests that it has weakened marriage and the intact, two-parent family and thereby damaged our social well-being, especially that of women and children. We cannot go back in history, but it seems time to establish some guidelines for the practice of cohabitation and to seriously question the further institutionalization of this new family form.

In place of institutionalizing cohabitation, in our opinion, we should be trying to revitalize marriage—not along classic male-dominant lines but along modern egalitarian lines. Particularly helpful in this regard would be educating young people about marriage from the early school years onward, getting them to make the wisest choices in their lifetime mates, and stressing the importance of long-term commitment to marriages. Such an educational venture could build on the fact that a huge majority of our nation's young people still express the strong desire to be in a long-term monogamous marriage.

These ideas are offered to the American public and especially to society's leaders in the spirit of generating a discussion. Our conclusions are tentative, and certainly not the last word on the subject. There is an obvious need for more research on cohabitation, and the findings of new research, of course, could alter our thinking. What is most important now, in our view, is a national debate on a topic that heretofore has been overlooked. Indeed, few issues seem more critical for the future of marriage and for generations to come.

"Contraception compromises the intimacy between husband and wife because it negates part of their being; in particular, that which is ordered to procreation."

Contraception Compromises Marital Intimacy

Donald DeMarco

In the following viewpoint, Donald DeMarco contends that because the use of contraception is an expression of self-interest, it blocks the unselfish intimacy that should exist between husband and wife. The act of preventing conception by unnatural means, he argues, is usually a couple's attempt to exert control over their lives by limiting the number of children they have. However, this attempt at control is based on an egoistic desire for a certain lifestyle or standard of living—self-centered needs that interfere with genuine intimacy. Only conjugal love that is unfettered by the self-interest evident in the use of contraception leads to true marital harmony and societal well-being, the author maintains. DeMarco is a philosophy professor at St. Jerome's University in Waterloo, Ontario, Canada, and author of several books, including *New Perspectives on Contraception*.

As you read, consider the following questions:

1. In DeMarco's opinion, what problems in American society are connected to contraception?
2. According to the author, what physiological benefits are derived from sexual intercourse without contraception?
3. What does the word *yadoah* refer to, according to DeMarco?

Excerpted from "Contraception and Compromised Intimacy," by Donald DeMarco, *New Oxford Review*, September 1998. Copyright ©1998 New Oxford Review. Reprinted with permission from *New Oxford Review* (1069 Kains Ave., Berkeley, CA 94706).

W hat is contraception? Is it the exercise of freedom and the acceptance of responsibility, as some claim? Or is contraception the illusion of freedom and avoidance of responsibility, as we are warned by the Catholic Church? What about contraception in marriage, specifically? Is it an aid to the controlled development of a free and loving relationship between two adult equals? Or is it a barrier to the intimacy that a man and woman called to the vocation of married love are meant to build? No answer can be attempted until we first grasp the relation between freedom and love.

Love Guides Freedom

If freedom simply means separation from others, or pure individuality, then love would actually hinder freedom. But without love, man is in a state of misery. Therefore, the freedom man seeks cannot exist without love. Love guides and directs freedom to what is good. To love another person means to use one's freedom in the interest of securing the other person's good. In this sense, freedom is not a terminal value but something that allows a good to be realized.

Contraception compromises the intimacy between husband and wife because it negates part of their being; in particular, that which is ordered to procreation. Another way of expressing this "compromise" is to say that the unselfishness of their spousal love is diluted by the presence of self-interest. Some secular philosophers argue that such self-interest is not subversive of love. Elizabeth Badinter, in *The Unopposite Sex: The End of the Gender Battle*, states that "the categorical imperative no longer sets out the conditions of the relationship between Ego and Other People, but those of my relationship with myself. It orders me to love myself, to develop myself, to enjoy myself." Contraception is consistent with this withdrawal into the self. Pope Paul VI fully recognized this shift toward the Ego and wrote sadly of the radical under-appreciation of love it presupposes:

> In love there is infinitely more than love. We would say that in human love there is divine love. And that is why the link between love and fecundity is deep, hidden, and substantial! All authentic love between a man and a woman, when it is not egoistic love, tends toward creation of another being issuing from that love. To love can mean "to love oneself," and

often love is no more than a juxtaposition of two solitudes. But when one has passed beyond that stage of egoism, when one has truly understood that love is shared joy, a mutual gift, then one comes to what is *truly* love.

"Juxtaposition of two solitudes" is a most poignant phrase, capturing the contradiction of performing an act designed to bring about unity, while one remains always able to fall back into one's isolated self. . . .

Contraception Trivializes Sex

Contraception allows sexual partners to go through the motions of being intimate without being truly intimate, that is, unreservedly and unconditionally so. The fact that contraception is perfectly in accord with the dominant tone of an alienated society means that the general populace scarcely notices its intrusion upon their intimacy, and seems unaware of contraception's connection to the trivialization of sex, the weakening of marriage, the increase in infidelity, and the dependence on abortion. As a young woman wrote to Dear Abby: "I am a twenty-three-year-old liberated woman who has been on the Pill for two years. It's getting pretty expensive and I think my boyfriend should share half the cost, but I don't know him well enough to discuss money with him."

This "liberated" woman apparently can communicate better with a stranger than she can with her "lover." She is oblivious to her own inner alienation, to the chasm between her verbal and sexual modes of communication. What appears to bother her most is not that her personality is in disarray, not that her claimed liberation may be illusory, not even that her most intimate companion is a person who does not know her—it bothers her that she is paying too much for contraception.

A self divided like this is not a candidate for a unified relationship. Self-division has no potential for intimacy with another. But in this world of alienation the threat to the self is still thought to come from outside, from "the other."

Bonding vs. Bondage

An intimate bond with another is not welcomed as a salutary form of bonding but is feared as a form of bondage. Central to a philosophy of individualism is the notion that intimacy between two people compromises individuality. The bond of matrimony is regarded as a form of bondage, and pregnancy is seen as more binding still. Contraception promises to liberate sexual partners from such bondage. But this method of preventing bondage also inhibits bonding.

Contraception is meant to free persons from their bodies while they use their bodies. But the body is an integral part of the human identity. It is primarily through the body that we are who we are and know others as they are. It is through the body that we meet others. A freedom dependent upon liberation from the body is essentially antihuman. Contemporary artists . . . call our attention to the existential plight of modern man, who is separated from community (isolation), from tradition (dislocation), from persons (alienation), from meaning (emptiness), and from hope (despair). Collectively these various separations can create an unhinderedness that gives the illusion of freedom. This freedom, however, is a freedom from the very elements of humanization. "You are not free unless you are bound," as the philosopher Karl Jaspers exclaims. A tree is not free to be itself if it is blocked from the sun, shorn of leaves, or uprooted from the soil. It must be bound to what feeds and sustains it.

Contraception Is Divisive

A divided self is less than whole. Therefore, he is less happy and is less able to give everything he is. Contraception, in separating baby-making from love-making, is divisive of the self. But it also diminishes what the marriage partners are able to bring to each other. Contraception is neither a boon to the self or to marriage.

Donald DeMarco, *Culture Wars*, June 1998.

Artists can dramatize our plight. It is the task of philosophers to clarify it, to make distinctions that show that bonding is not the same as bondage. Bondage is restricting and frustrating, contrary to one's natural needs, in no way compatible with freedom. Bonding, on the other hand, if it is directed by love to a good, can be the beginning of an expanding freedom. Bonding is an adherence to that which overcomes our isolation and alienation and completes us.

Bondage and bonding do have something in common: Both involve connectedness. But bondage is stifling, a connection with something that hinders. Bonding can be liberating if it is interpersonal and protected by love: Friendship, for instance, is a bond that we cannot do without. The philosopher Benedict Spinoza understood bondage to be the consequence of making desire absolute—a consequence I find vividly dramatized in, for example, Somerset Maugham's novel *Of Human Bondage*, a portrait of the enslaving potential of sexual lust.

Physiological Bonding

There is no disputing the fact that bondage can exist. Bonding is far more subtle and mysterious, but the evidence for its existence is decisive. Bonding between humans includes emotional, moral, and spiritual dimensions, of course, but even a materialistic analysis shows that interpersonal bonding can be authenticated on a biochemical level, where it appears in its most natural and spontaneous form. There are essentially three kinds of such biochemical bonding between humans: sexual intercourse, pregnancy, and lactation. Each of these is related to the next in such a way as to promote the development of the child *and* the relationship between the parents. Biochemical bonding is not only compatible with developing freedom but is its very condition—its soil and sun.

It is well established, scientifically, that both male and female derive physiological benefits from the absorption of the other's secretions during sexual union. The assimilation by the male of hormones that the female organs pass to the man's body through the permeable mucous membranes of the male organ, and the assimilation by the female of the semen and its hormones through her mucous membranes, play an important role in the physical and emotional processes that contribute to a harmonious married life.

Dr. Marie Stopes recognized early in the 20th century that a woman suffers a loss of well-being when deprived of her husband's seminal and prostatic fluid. She reported her findings, which were later corroborated by other medical researchers, in 1919 in her book *Wise Parenthood*. She opposed *coitus interruptus* and the use of the condom precisely because they deprive the sexual act of its full physiological value. Sexual intercourse is ordered to physical ends other than simply procreation even on a physiological level. It confers on the partners a multitude of benefits that all contribute in their own way to facilitating the special bond of unity between husband and wife that is the bond of matrimony.

Compromised Intimacy

Sexual union is a two-in-one-flesh intimacy that requires the complete surrender of the spouses to each other. Even materially—biochemically—contraception compromises this intimacy. Emotionally and spiritually, too, contraception is a way of holding back, of not giving everything one has and not accepting all that the other is. Those who employ contraception usually do so (they claim) in the interest of gaining some measure of control over their lives. But the control gained is somewhat illusory, since it usually implies a willingness to give oneself to something other than the marriage. Spouses often compromise their marital intimacy so that they do not compromise their intimacy with something else: This other "intimacy" is frequently a certain standard of living or style of living with which children—they fear—will interfere.

A contracepting couple may not recognize the subtle erosions that their capitulation to fear, anxiety, and autonomy can bring about. They may be convinced that they are agreeing to use contraception, that they share this value. Yet clearly a seemingly intimate agreement to avert intimacy will not yield intimacy in the end.

The family is the basic unit of society. More fundamentally, marriage is the basis of the family. Even more fundamentally, a loving, intimate union of husband and wife is the basis of a good marriage. Therefore, the uncompromised intimacy between spouses establishes a solid foundation for society. A good marriage, as ethicist William E. May asserts, is the "rock on which the family is built." "Children can flourish fully," he states, "only in the family rooted in the marriage of one man and woman. Only if this truth is recognized can a 'civilization of love' be developed.". . .

A Knowing Intimacy

The Old Testament uses the word *yadoah* ("knowing") for the act of sexual union. Knowledge and sexual love have an important factor in common in that they both imply an entering into something that exists outside the self. The knower is united with the known, and his knowledge is objective to the degree it is free from subjective prejudices and biases. The true knower knows his beloved as she is and not as he might prefer her to be. Likewise, the true lover will love his partner as she is, without altering her being to suit some convenience or security need of his. In this same sense, the ancients proclaimed, *ubi amor, ibi oculus*—where there is love, there is vision (knowledge).

By taking knowing and loving together—*yadoah*—a special intimacy is achieved between husband and wife in which each knows and loves the other with reverence; that is, with respect for the true nature of the other. This *yadoah* intimacy is the basis for creativity in the married life of husband and wife, in the life of the species, and in the continuing life of the community. As Ida Görres has written, "marriage is the hallowed ground, the sanctified place for those lovers who should, who are able, who are permitted and who are determined to take the risk of procreation."

"Contraception did not . . . lead me to lose respect for my wife, nor lead her to feel used."

Contraception Does Not Compromise Marital Intimacy

James Nuechterlein

In the following viewpoint, James Nuechterlein argues that the use of contraception does not create barriers to intimacy between husband and wife. Moreover, he maintains, among Christians, a majority of Protestants and many Catholics believe that it is moral and reasonable to practice most forms of contraception. Every act of conjugal union need not be procreative for husband and wife to have a healthy, loving relationship, Nuechterlein contends. Nuechterlein is the editor of *First Things*, a monthly journal focusing on religion and public life.

As you read, consider the following questions:
1. What concerns were addressed in the 1968 *Humanae Vitae*?
2. Why did the author and his wife not want to have children immediately after they were married?
3. What is natural law, according to Nuechterlein?

Reprinted, with permission, from "Catholics, Protestants, and Contraception," by James Nuechterlein, *First Things*, April 1999.

It has become a commonplace that religious controversy today occurs more often across church boundaries than between them. Prior to Vatican II [a reform movement in the Catholic Church initiated in the early 1960s], the most important theological disputes in America—and in the West in general—pitted Protestants against Catholics. In the decades since, such disputes have increasingly pitted religious traditionalists against religious progressives—with diminishing regard, on either side, to denominational affiliation. In shorthand terms, the present division separates those who see the creeds as expressions of truth from those who see them as exercises in metaphor.

Differences between Catholics and Protestants have not entirely disappeared, of course. Papal infallibility and the Marian dogmas come immediately to mind, as does the issue of the ordination of women. But on most matters of faith and practice—including abortion, the great socioreligious issue of our time—conservative Catholics and Protestants stand together in opposition to their liberal coreligionists.

The Issue of Contraception

There is one great exception to this contemporary reconfiguration of religious alignments: the issue of contraception. Conservative Protestants may share Pope Paul VI's concerns in *Humanae Vitae* (1968) about the overall negative effects of ready access to birth control on sexual morality. But virtually none of them—as evidenced, for example, in the *First Things* symposium on contraception in December 1998—is ready to go along with the Catholic Church's insistence that each and every conjugal act must be open to procreation. The Pope's prescient consequentialist arguments against contraception do not, in Protestant eyes, outlaw its legitimate use within a marriage open to children.

There are divisions within Catholicism on this point: Many Catholics, it is clear, do not practice what the Church teaches. But among Protestants, it is not simply that the overwhelming majority of them come down on the same side of the issue, but that for most of them *there is no real issue here at all. . . .*

Permit me a personal elaboration. When my wife and I

married, we assumed as a matter of course that we would have children. She talked about eight; I thought two would be fine, but indicated a willingness to negotiate. (We wound up, in the end, with three.) We did not want children immediately—I was still in graduate school—but if she had become pregnant, we would not for a moment have considered abortion.

But neither for a moment did we morally hesitate to practice contraception. (The only extended discussion was over the method.) It was not a matter of carefully weighing the pros and cons and struggling to a decision. We no more debated whether we would use contraception than we debated whether we would, in the fullness of time, have children. Of course we would someday, God willing, have children; of course, in the meantime, we would practice (non-abortifacient) contraception. This was not, for us, a matter of presuming on God's providence. It seemed rather a right use of reason in fulfilling the various goods of our marriage.

Contraception Does Not Create Emotional Barriers

It is important to emphasize, further, that at no time did contraception create a moral or emotional barrier between us. (We have recently discussed this at some length.) We always reached agreement on when we would use it and when not, and during the times we did, it was never, logistics occasionally aside, in any way a difficulty. Whatever problems arose in our marriage, contraception was never among them. Contraception did not, contrary to the warnings of *Humanae Vitae* on this point, lead me to lose respect for my wife, nor lead her to feel used. If someone had told us, in the words of one *First Things* correspondent, that we were "withholding our fertility from one another," he would have met with blank incomprehension. We intended both the unitive and procreative goods of marriage, but not necessarily both in every act of love.

The point of this self-revelation is not to insist on the rightness of our view of these matters. It is rather to suggest how utterly typical that view was and is. There is nothing singular in our experience, I believe; it is, mutatis mutandis, the experience of most Protestant couples of our generation and after. And I am speaking not of liberal Protestants, but of Protestants committed to a thoroughly orthodox understanding of Christian faith and life. We are as conventional and conservative on issues of sexual morality as our most traditionalist Catholic friends. But while we do not oppose natural family planning—indeed we find it admirable—we cannot concede that it is the only licit method of regulating fertility.

Natural Law

Catholic/Protestant differences on contraception matter as much as they do because they are entangled with larger issues. The Catholic position on contraception, at least as traditionally formulated, is based on natural law. Natural law does not depend on biblical revelation or dogmatic formulation. Its precepts, according to Thomistic understanding, are planted in the hearts of all people and are accessible by reason. We are dealing here, in J. Budziszewski's nice phrase, with those moral laws "we can't not know."

Contraception Provides Benefits

The use of birth control by married couples can be a great blessing. It permits them time to grow in greater love and commitment at the beginning of a marriage, and to prepare themselves for the great task of parenthood. It is difficult to believe that nonabortifacient forms of birth control are intrinsically evil, for if they were, surely they would produce evil results in the couples that use them; and yet there are very many spouses who employ contraception with only beneficial results.

Sarah E. Hinlicky, *First Things*, December 1998.

Natural law has never played as large a role in Protestant theology as it has among Catholic thinkers. Some Protestants, in the tradition of Karl Barth, vigorously oppose it; for others its role is marginal. But most conservative Protestants take natural law seriously, and see it as an essential element in maintaining public moral standards in an increasingly pluralistic culture.

Enter contraception. Paul VI addressed *Humanae Vitae* not just to Catholics but "to all men of good will," thus suggesting its foundation in a natural law argument presumably readily available to non-Catholics. But, it turns out, the prohibition against contraception is—for Protestants—a moral law they *can* "not know." This raises problems, possibly for Protestants, certainly for our understanding of natural law.

Aquinas conceded that there are situations where some people under some circumstances can be blinded to natural law precepts. It seems odd to suppose, however, that in our time virtually all Protestants (and not a few Catholics) would have their moral faculties so corrupted—not in general, but on this one particular issue. And the problem cannot be attributed to lack of careful consideration. Many serious Protestants have by now read and pondered *Humanae Vitae* and remain as unpersuaded by its arguments as do those who have never given it a moment's thought. Positions on this issue are firmly set. . . .

The point of my argument, again, is not—or not primarily—to insist that Protestants have this matter right. I obviously think they do, but this is not the occasion to attempt fully to establish that. The point is rather to remind orthodox Christians, Catholic and Protestant alike, that we have in contraception and issues that flow from it an impediment perhaps more formidable than we like to suppose to the ecumenical fellowship that is, for so many of us, our deepest longing. In *Humanae Vitae* Paul VI noted, in magnificent understatement, that "it is to be anticipated that perhaps not everyone will easily accept this particular teaching." On that, thirty years down the line, we can all agree. The question is where we go from there.

Periodical Bibliography

The following articles have been selected to supplement the diverse views presented in this chapter. Addresses are provided for periodicals not indexed in the *Readers' Guide to Periodical Literature*, the *Alternative Press Index*, the *Social Sciences Index*, or the *Index to Legal Periodicals and Books*.

Economist	"Sexual Mores: Come Live with Me," February 6, 1999.
Kate Fillion	"This Is the Sexual Revolution," *Saturday Night*, February 1996.
Maggie Gallagher	"Dust Off Those Old Sexual Rules," *Conservative Chronicle*, May 19, 1999. Available from Box 29, Hampton, IA 50441.
Health and Sexuality	Special issue on the health benefits of contraception, Fall 1996. Available from the Association of Reproductive Health Professionals, 2401 Pennsylvania Ave. NW, Ste. 350, Washington, DC 20037.
Craig Lasher	"Playing with People's Lives," *Free Inquiry*, Spring 1999. Available from 3965 Rensch Rd., Amherst, NY 14228-2713.
John Leland and Mark Miller	"Can Gays 'Convert'?" *Newsweek*, August 17, 1998.
Thomas Lickona	"Ten Consequences of Premature Sexual Involvement," *U.S. Catholic*, April 1996.
Connie Marshner	"The Modern Dating Game Is Rigged Against Players," *Insight*, September 29, 1997. Available from 3600 New York Ave. NE, Washington, DC 20002.
Marianne Means	"Birth Control Under Attack," *Liberal Opinion*, July 20, 1998. Available from 108 E. Fifth St., Vinton, IA 52349.
Charles E. Moore	"Preparing Young People for Marital Fidelity," *New Oxford Review*, March 1999. Available from 1029 Kains Ave., Berkeley, CA 94706.
Thomas Moore	"The Marriage Bed," *New Age*, special issue: The Annual Guide to Holistic Living 1999. Available from PO Box 1949, Marion, OH 43305-1949.
Linda J. Waite	"The Importance of Marriage Is Being Overlooked," *USA Today*, January 1, 1999.
Pat Wingert	"I Do, I Do—Maybe," *Newsweek*, November 2, 1998.

CHAPTER 3

How Should Sex Education Be Conducted?

Chapter Preface

In 1996, Congress authorized the use of federal funds for state-run programs that encourage teens to remain sexually abstinent until marriage. As of 1997, participating states have used the funding in various ways: Some have given grants to community organizations that promote youth abstinence; others use the money for media campaigns that encourage parents to discuss sex with their children. Most states have, in fact, split the federal money among several approaches. But some have opted to use all the funding to revamp public-school sex education curricula. By 1999, for example, five states had passed laws requiring public schools to teach that the societal norm for sexual activity is "mutually faithful monogamous heterosexual relationships in the context of marriage." Parents, educators, and public health advocates have had mixed reactions to the implementation of abstinence-centered education in schools.

Joe S. McIlhaney Jr., president of the Medical Institute for Sexual Health, contends that the best sex education programs stress youth abstinence. Given the proliferation of out-of-wedlock births and sexually transmitted diseases in the past few decades, he argues, schools have a duty to promote abstinence as the only sure way for teens to avoid pregnancy or disease. In his view, teaching students "safer sex" techniques, such as the use of condoms, is irresponsible because condoms are not 100 percent risk-free. "[Students] must not leave the . . . classroom thinking, 'I'm being responsible and safe if I use a condom,'" insists McIlhaney. "The school's message must be unmistakably clear: 'There is no responsible sex for unmarried teenagers.'"

Debra W. Haffner, president of the Sexuality Information and Education Council, disputes McIlhaney's contentions. Sex education, she argues, should include a broad range of information that helps youths "develop the skills to resist peer pressure, set sexual limits and negotiate the use of contraceptives and condoms." Haffner maintains that abstinence-only curricula present an unrealistic and negative view of premarital sex and contraception. "The majority of people have sexual relations prior to marriage with no negative repercussions," she points out. Rather than exaggerating the possible harmful consequences of sexual behavior, sex education should teach youths "to delay sexual activity or else protect themselves."

These conflicting approaches to sex education are examined by the authors of the following viewpoints as they debate what sexual values schools should emphasize.

1

"Studies reveal that teenagers who partake in discussions that include all options, from chastity belts to condoms, often delay sexual intercourse or reduce its frequency."

Schools Should Emphasize Comprehensive Sex Education

Carolyn Mackler

Students should receive a sex education that emphasizes a balanced and positive approach to sexuality and sexual behavior, maintains Carolyn Mackler in the following viewpoint. This approach, often referred to as comprehensive sex education, encourages students to delay having sex but also teaches them about human development, birth control, pregnancy, STD prevention, intimacy, and sexual pleasure. Mackler contends that the government-backed alternatives to comprehensive sex education—abstinence-only programs—generate fear of sexuality and leave students misinformed about contraceptive options, STDs, and other aspects of sexual behavior. Comprehensive sex education, however, enables students to make responsible and healthy decisions regarding sexuality. Mackler is a contributing editor of the feminist magazine *Ms.*

As you read, consider the following questions:

1. According to Mackler, what percentage of U.S. schoolchildren receive sex education similar to the program offered at Ridgewood High School?
2. In Mackler's opinion, what is the nature of the "Great Antipleasure Conspiracy"?
3. What is the guiding principle of comprehensive sexuality education, according to the author?

The 12:55 bell rings at Ridgewood High School and a flock of freshmen filter into Evelyn Rosskamm Shalom's Health 9 class. Greeting the sea of navy blue baseball caps and Capri pants, Shalom announces that today's lesson will commence with the "question box" and instructs students to proceed as quietly as possible to the Magic Carpet. In a stampede evocative of July in Pamplona, 25 pairs of Nikes and clunky sandals clamor onto a dingy gray rug at the back of the room and, with one brave male exception, self-segregate by gender: girls on one side, boys on the other, a puerile triad huddled in the back. Shalom, joking about her recent fiftieth birthday, treats herself to a metal chair at the mouth of the circle and produces slips of folded, white paper.

"Any more to add before I begin?" she asks, casually tucking a wayward strand of auburn hair behind one ear.

Braces-revealing smirks ripple through the crowd, especially among the Peanut Gallery trio, who menacingly ooze "spitball" from every pore of their bodies.

Shalom quickly scans a crumpled selection. "Have I already answered: 'Why do people have oral sex?'"

The Peanut Gallery erupts and a handful of mid-pubescents dutifully nod their heads. Shalom, a 16-year veteran of Ridgewood High School who has been described as someone who rules a class with velvet-gloved discipline, allows the rascals a heartbeat to blow off steam before skillfully channeling their discomfort into a lively debate in response to the next question: "What is the right age to have sex?" Once Shalom takes the floor to address the query, a hush falls over the Magic Carpet. The only discernable sound is the buzzing of florescent lights above. Fifty eyes are intent on Shalom. Even the Peanut Gallery is hooked.

Sex Education at Ridgewood High

So goes a typical health class at Ridgewood High School in suburban New Jersey. The Ridgewood school district is renowned for its comprehensive and thorough family-life education curriculum. Following a 1980 statewide mandate that all New Jersey schoolchildren were to have sex education, Ridgewood Public Schools formed an advisory committee to consult with the school regarding its ever-evolving curriculum. Ridgewood students receive health education every year of their public school careers, beginning with instruction from a certified nurse specialist in elementary school and progressing to classes taught by high school teachers, such as Shalom, who has a master's degree in health education.

"Ridgewood takes it seriously," Shalom explains, sipping a raspberry Snapple after class. "We have a minister, a pediatrician, someone from the YMCA, several parents, and two students, among others, serving on the committee, which reviews everything that will go on in my class, from lessons to controversial videos. I'm under more scrutiny than the English teacher, but by the same token, I have a support network. If a parent calls to complain—which happens infrequently—I'm not out on a limb by myself."

And then there's the question box, or anonymous questions, as they're often referred to in health-education circles. Shalom operates her question box—a pushing-the-envelope trade tool that gives the teacher jurisdiction to answer any inquiry—by first distributing identical slips of paper and then requiring that all students write one to three lines. (If a student has no question, she or he must thrice scribble "I have no questions at the present time.") And finally, Shalom makes good on her promise to honor every question, which in any given session can produce such gems as "Do teenagers have sex?" "Is it right to have an abortion if you get pregnant by mistake?" and "What exactly do guys do when they masturbate?" Shalom notes, "In any class, if someone is asking a question, you know that at least a few other people were wondering the same thing." She informs her students from the start not to waste time devising outrageous queries just to get a reaction; she's been at this too long to get embarrassed. And with no further ado, she plows into the explanation minefield with nary a blush.

Perhaps it's the ubiquitous fluorescent lights that stir up decade-old memories of my eleventh-grade health class, where the beefy, small-town wrestling coach slapped transparencies of the chlamydia bacterium onto the overhead projector and recited a litany of drippy symptoms, in a lesson that bore a greater resemblance to the previous year's fetal pig dissection than to my forays in the back of minivans. As I recount my tale of sex ed woe, Shalom shakes her head. "If kids are going to change their behavior, we need to teach them the facts before they engage, but that alone is not sufficient. We must give them time to talk about their attitudes and practice communication skills." Pushing her wire-rimmed glasses up on her nose, she adds, "Anyway, Ridgewood would never make a physical education teacher cover chlamydia, just as they wouldn't expect me to coach volleyball."

A Politically Explosive Issue

Fade from the Magic Carpet to a school district in Franklin County, North Carolina, where, in the fall of 1997, a scissors-toting parent-volunteer was summoned to the high school to slice chapters 17, 20, and 21 out of ninth-graders' health text-books. The culpable text—covering contraception, sexually transmitted diseases (STDs), and relationships—didn't comply with the statewide abstinence-only curriculum, ruled the school board. Apparently, in a state where in 1996 there were 25,240 recorded pregnancies among 15- to 19-year-olds, the board hoped that if they obliterated a discourse on condoms, getting down wouldn't dawn on youngsters.

Unfortunately, this sort of scene is business as usual with the politically explosive issue of school-based sex education. While a uniform national curriculum does not exist, barrels of federal money are being siphoned into abstinence-only-until-marriage programs, frequently laden with wrath-of-God scare tactics. Comprehensive sexuality education the likes of Ridgewood's, designed to reinforce sexuality as a positive and healthy part of being human, is available to only about 5 percent of schoolchildren in the United States. Sexuality education is an across-the-school-boards contentious subject, bound to generate controversy, even among well-meaning feminists; sexuality is not a one-size-fits-all equation, and the messages appropriate for one kid may not work for the girl or boy at the adjacent desk.

And then there's the Great Antipleasure Conspiracy. Translation: adults swindling kids (especially girls) by trying to convince them that sex is no fun, in the hope that they won't partake, a practice exemplified by the shocking omission of the clitoris—whose sole function is to deliver female pleasure—from most high school biology textbooks. The notion of women experiencing erotic pleasure—or possessing full sexual agency—clearly scares the boxer shorts off conservative educators. Analogous to attempting to eradicate pizza by withholding Italy from a map of Europe, not including the clitoris in a textbook depiction of female genitalia is a frighteningly misleading excuse for education.

© Kirk Anderson. Reprinted with permission.

Tiptoeing around any of these issues—from pleasure to power to pregnancy prevention—is denying youngsters their basic right to health information. It is catapulting them into life-threatening sexual scenarios without sufficient tools to protect themselves. It is jeopardizing their chance to lay sturdy foundations for a sexually healthy adulthood. It's time to wake up and smell the hormones.

Ridgewood boasts one of the most progressive school districts in a "mixed landscape," explains Susan N. Wilson, the executive coordinator of the Network for Family Life Education, a nonprofit organization based at the Rutgers School for Social Work in Piscataway, New Jersey, that promotes comprehensive sexuality education in schools and communities. Wilson, whom Shalom calls a "crusader for sexuality education," explains that over the past several years there has been progress in the quantity of sex education in the schools. "In most places, it exists; something is being taught," she says, "but there are many school districts where students receive the bare minimum—HIV education—and very, very late in their school lives." Wilson points out that many politicians have embraced AIDS education with open arms. "In a true intertwining of church and state, they've jumped at the chance to reveal that sex does, in fact, equal death."

Fear-Based Abstinence Programs

Debra Haffner, president of the Sexuality Information and Education Council of the United States (SIECUS), a nonprofit group that advocates for sexuality education and sexual rights, describes how most young people in this country get hurried through sex-abuse prevention in early grade school, the Puberty Talk in fifth grade, a lesson on HIV and STDs in middle school, and possibly a health elective in high school. "There's currently a great emphasis on abstinence in this country," she adds, "partially driven by federal programs, but partially driven by the conservative influence in communities."

Seasoned feminist sexuality educators consistently encourage teenagers to postpone intercourse until they're prepared for a mature sexual relationship. But the puritanical monsoon of fear-based abstinence education swamping the country is a different matter. As part of welfare reform in 1996, Congress passed, and President Clinton signed into law, a federal program that allocates cash—a total of $50 million per fiscal year—to states that teach abstinence-only-until-marriage as the expected standard for school-age children. The modus operandi of these programs is to highlight the "harmful psychological and physical effects" of premarital and extramarital sexual activity and erase any discourse on contraceptives—which curiously ignores the notion that abstainers-until-marriage may, in fact, want to utilize birth control once they've tied the connubial knot.

Abstinence-only lessons, though varying from classroom to classroom, often revolve around a "pet your dog, not your date" theme. One resoundingly sexist message is that the onus of restricting foreplay should fall on the girl, encouraging her to use "self-control" rather than "birth control." A pseudoscientific chart from Sex Respect, a fear-based abstinence curriculum, depicts how male genitalia become aroused during "necking," while female genitalia lag behind until "petting." The girl-cum-gatekeeper's pleasure gets swept to the side, leaving her to ward filthy, boys-will-be-boys paws off her silky drawers.

In many fear-based abstinence lessons, misinformation abounds. One curriculum emphasizes the "danger" of French kissing by falsely implying that the concentration of HIV in saliva is high enough to be transmitted via spit-swapping. Mum is the word from teachers in response to students whose queries flirt with anything other than the abstinence-only model. In a public-school-aired video entitled *No Second Chance* (Jeremiah Films), a student demands of a nurse: "What if I want to have sex before I get married?" Her chilling response: "I guess you just have to be prepared to die . . . and take your spouse and one or more of your children with you."

The Dangers of Abstinence-Only Education

The overwhelming bulk of scientific research underscores the failure of abstinence-only education in doing anything but eclipsing the erotic with the neurotic. A recent report by the National Campaign to Prevent Teen Pregnancy revealed that "the weight of the current evidence indicates that these abstinence programs do not delay the onset of intercourse." In a country where a mere 6.9 percent of men and 21 percent of women ages 18 to 59 hold out for their honeymoon, force-feeding "Just Say No" to teenagers sends them scurrying to the playground or onto the Web in search of information—usually to find misinformation—and frolicking under the covers all the same. But the risks of leaving kids without sufficient skills and facts range from the obvious—pregnancy and STDs—to sexual abuse, date rape, and sexual powerlessness.

Reducing adolescent pregnancy and the risk of sexually transmitted diseases is clearly paramount. But Susan Wilson, who's convinced that the right wants to "stamp out" teen sexuality altogether, wonders whether the effort is "on a collision course with healthy sexuality."

Debra Haffner echoes similar sentiments. "My mentor from 20 years ago used to call that 'Sex is dirty. Save it for someone you love,'" she scoffs. "We cannot ingrain in young people the message that sexual intercourse violates another person, kills people, and leaves you without a reputation, and then expect that the day they put a wedding band on their finger they're going to forget all that."

She pauses and adds wryly, "It just creates adults who are in sex therapy because they can't have fulfilling relationships with their spouses and partners."

Comprehensive Sexuality Education

"Hearing the term 'sex ed,' people think of plumbing lessons and organ recitals," proclaims Haffner. "They envision anatomy and physiology and disaster prevention. Sexuality education, on the other hand, underscores that sexuality is about who we are, as women and men, not what we do with one certain part of our bodies."

In 1996, SIECUS published the second edition of its *Guidelines for Comprehensive Sexuality Education: K–12*, which it had originally developed earlier in the decade with a task force that included the Centers for Disease Control and Prevention, Planned Parenthood Federation of America, and the National School Boards Association. The guidelines serve as a framework to facilitate the development of a comprehensive sex education program arising from the belief that "young people explore their sexuality as a natural process of achieving sexual maturity." Accordingly, emphasis should be placed on informed decision-making about intercourse by acknowledging—not condemning—the broad range of adolescent sexual behaviors.

The SIECUS sexuality education model is designed to spiral through the school years, with age-appropriate lessons at all grade levels. Starting in early elementary school, children would learn, among many things, proper terminology for female and male genitalia. "When I tell this to my seniors," Shalom explains, referring to the students in her elective course on parenting, "they are shocked. They say, 'But then you'll have little kids singing "vulva, vulva, vulva" all day long.' And I point out that three-year-olds don't run around saying 'shoulder, shoulder, shoulder.' It should just be part of their whole repertoire."

The philosophy behind comprehensive sexuality education is to start small with all concepts relating to sexuality and add on as children's developmental capabilities mature. If the topic is sexual identity, in upper elementary school, 9- to 12-year-olds (already having defined homosexuality in previous grades) would learn about anti-gay discrimination and add bisexuality to the mixing pot. By junior high, students learn theories behind the determination of sexual orientation and discuss same-sex fantasies. Unfortunately, this approach to homosexuality is to sex education what simultaneous multiple orgasms are to sex—rare. Even in progressive school districts, discourse on sexual orientation remains painfully patchy, often providing little insight and appearing very late.

Proponents of comprehensive sexuality education believe that by high school, teenagers should have processed enough information to make responsible choices surrounding sex. And the research is on their side: studies reveal that teenagers who partake in discussions that include all options, from chastity belts to condoms, often delay sexual intercourse or reduce its frequency. By cultivating in adolescents a sense of sexual self-determination—with empowerment and gratification and honest communication being central—things tend to fall into place; unwanted pregnancy and sexually transmitted diseases remain on the periphery, not at the hub of their ideas about human sexuality.

Acknowledging a Range of Sexual Values

Back to the Great Antipleasure Conspiracy. There's reluctance even among liberal adults—most likely due to their own discomfort surrounding sexuality—to acknowledge that the majority of sex is for recreation, not procreation. Scarier still is the notion of pleasuring oneself. Wilson points out that masturbation is a subject "avoided assiduously by teachers." It is essential for schools to employ educators who will not blanch at the mention of, say, a clitoris (and who, like Shalom, boycott clitoris-free textbooks). "Nobody invests money in training," says Wilson, who points out that often sex ed teachers hit the chalkboard with only a weekend workshop under their belt. "A basic course in human sexuality for everyone in the helping professions should be commonplace."

Sex education can even send shivers up feminist spines when it comes to handling a controversial issue like abortion. It seems easy if the teacher is pro-choice; explosive if she or he boasts a bumper sticker broadcasting "Abortion Stops a Beating Heart!" The safest way to navigate this tangled terrain is for teachers to acknowledge the range of values surrounding issues such as homosexuality, abortion, or masturbation in the hope that students will ultimately develop their own, educated opinions. "If there were a school-based program that only presented the pro-choice point of view, that would be wrong," says Haffner, who has recently published a SIECUS monograph, *A Time to Speak: Faith Communities and Sexuality Education*, in which she emphasizes the role of religious institutions in the education of their young congregants and encourages churches and synagogues to coordinate their curricula with those of the schools.

Another key means for schools to negotiate the values quagmire is to give credence to SIECUS' omnipresent message that parents should be the primary sexuality educators. Envisioning a proliferation of parent nights, when parents could meet the health teachers and review the material, Haffner encourages educators to solicit parental support, all in the hope that the classroom will serve as a catalyst for domestic dialogue.

"Most Americans are terrified of this subject," says Wilson. "We teach people to read and we expect them to read. We teach people about numbers and we expect them to be able to do mathematical equations. So then we're saying we don't want to teach kids about human sexuality, but we're hoping they make sensible decisions?"

"I know I've done my job well," explains Shalom, "when a kid articulates to me, 'I never realized sex was so complicated until I took your class.' Not that it's bad. Not that it's evil. Not that it's nasty. But it's complicated, and maybe more than you want to get into at 14."

"Sexual abstinence among adolescents is the best choice for their physical, emotional, educational, and economic future."

Schools Should Emphasize Abstinence-Only Sex Education

National Coalition for Abstinence Education

The National Coalition for Abstinence Education (NCAE) is an alliance of sixty organizations dedicated to insuring the implementation of the Title V Abstinence Education Program, which was authorized by Congress in 1997. In the following viewpoint, the NCAE contends that schoolchildren should learn that abstinence from nonmarital sexual activity is the societal norm. Educators should teach that abstinence before marriage is the only sure way to avoid unwanted pregnancy, STDs, and various emotional problems related to premature sexual activity. Comprehensive sex education programs, on the other hand, teach that abstinence is simply one among several optional methods to avoid pregnancy and STDs. Such programs should be avoided, maintains the NCAE, because they give students mixed messages about appropriate sexual behavior.

As you read, consider the following questions:

1. According to the NCAE, what eight conditions should be met by abstinence-centered sex education programs?
2. How does the NCAE respond to the criticism that abstinence-centered education is "fear-based"?

There is considerable confusion about the federally funded Abstinence Education Program being implemented beginning in 1997. Unfortunately, certain groups that are opposed to the program are actively distributing misinformation in an attempt to undermine the program.

The purposes of this viewpoint are to answer the most commonly asked questions about the Title V Abstinence Education Program and to address the misinformation campaign being conducted by the program's opposition.

The Title V Abstinence Education Program

• *What is the Title V Abstinence Education Program?* As part of the welfare-reform act of 1996, Congress authorized $50 million of federal funds annually for five years to be provided to the states in the form of block grants to promote abstinence until marriage. When combined with required state matching funds of $3 for every $4 federal dollars, $437 million will be available to support the abstinence message during the duration of the program.

• *Doesn't the matching funds requirement place an undue burden on the states?* This argument is not factual. It is not unusual for federal programs to require state matching funds. Additionally, in many states not a single penny of state money will be used to meet the matching requirement. In some states, organizations such as curriculum providers will be required to find their own match. In other states, the match will be met with in-kind donations. In yet others, existing abstinence programs will qualify to satisfy the match. In fact, very few states are using actual state dollars to meet the matching requirement—and those states are doing so out of the conviction that abstinence education is greatly needed.

However, it is entirely fair to expect all states to provide at least a portion of the matching funds. After all, states provide funds to promote the comprehensive safe-sex message. Doesn't it make sense for states to support adolescents who have made a healthy choice for abstinence as well?

• *Doesn't the Title V abstinence money come with too many strings attached?* No more than usual conditions are placed on all block grants provided to the states. For example, highway funds may carry restrictions on speed limits, construction techniques, materials and so on.

The Title V program requires the states to fund education that:

1. has as its exclusive purpose, teaching the social, psychological and health gains to be realized by abstaining from sexual activity;
2. teaches abstinence from sexual activity outside marriage as the expected standard for all school-age children;
3. teaches that abstinence from sexual activity is the only certain way to avoid out-of-wedlock pregnancy, sexually transmitted diseases and other associated health problems;
4. teaches that a mutually faithful monogamous relationship in context of marriage is the expected standard of human sexual activity;
5. teaches that sexual activity outside of the context of marriage is likely to have harmful psychological and physical effects;
6. teaches that bearing children out of wedlock is likely to have harmful consequences for the child, the child's parents and society;
7. teaches young people how to reject sexual advances and how alcohol and drug use increases vulnerability to sexual advances; and
8. teaches the importance of attaining self sufficiency before engaging in sexual activity.

These eight conditions are entirely realistic and based on fact. As long as these conditions are satisfied, states are given great latitude in the implementation of abstinence programs.

• *But aren't the vast majority of students sexually active? Won't they have sex no matter what they're taught?* Wrong. Not everybody is doing it. In fact, in 1995 the federal Centers for Disease Control found that nearly half of high school students (48 percent of girls, 46 percent of boys) had *never* had a sexual experience. In addition, a large percentage of students who have had sex wish they had remained virgins— and would like to acquire the skills to become abstinent.

• *Doesn't this abstinence program take money away from other sexuality education programs?* Again, this is part of the misinformation campaign against the abstinence program. Not a single federal safe-sex program (such as Title X, Title XX, HIV/AIDS, etc.) has been defunded in order to make the Title V Abstinence Education Program available. The condom crowd has not lost a single penny. They just don't want any *other* approach to be given a fair chance.

• *Isn't $50 million per year a lot of money?* As citizens, we should be concerned about how our tax dollars are spent. But $50 million is a modest amount of money for a new approach to such a serious problem. It amounts to just $1.33 for each adolescent in the U.S. And $50 million is just a fraction of the amount spent to promote contraceptives as the solution to adolescent pregnancies and sexually transmitted diseases.

Over $6 BILLION (adjusted to current dollars) have been spent since 1971 to support Title X "safe-sex" education. Add to this other federal programs aimed at reducing the consequences of out-of-wedlock sexual promiscuity (such as HIV/AIDS programs, family planning, etc.) and hundreds of millions of dollars are spent each year to promote the comprehensive safe-sex message. And this does not include direct spending by states. For example, California alone will spend over $78 million in teen pregnancy prevention programs in Fiscal Year 1998, largely focused on the contraceptive message.

Considering that the combined social, medical and economic cost of adolescent sexual promiscuity is about $35 billion each year (direct and indirect costs), $50 million is a small price to encourage and equip the over 50 percent of America's youth ages 12 to 19 who have chosen abstinence and need our help to fulfill that choice.

Abstinence-Only vs. Abstinence-Plus

• *Don't comprehensive safe-sex education programs promote abstinence in a much more "balanced" manner?* Herein lies the key distinction between abstinence-centered sexuality education and comprehensive (abstinence-plus) safe-sex education.

The message of abstinence-centered sex education is as follows:

It is entirely possible for adolescents to remain abstinent. In fact, the majority of females ages 12 to 19 have never had sex. Health professionals agree that abstinence is, far and away, the single most healthy choice. But, to remain abstinent, teens need to be encouraged and equipped with medically and socially accurate information on the consequences of sexual promiscuity and with knowledge, character development and skills on how to remain abstinent. And abstinence needs to be presented in a manner which unapologetically states that choosing the best alternative in sexual health is the societal norm.

The message of comprehensive safe-sex education:

We'd prefer that you choose abstinence. But if you decide not to choose abstinence, make sure you use a condom.

A parallel message to abstinence-centered education would be this: "Don't smoke; it is not healthy for all the following reasons . . . and here are a number of skills to help you avoid smoking."

Bob Gorrell/*Richmond Times Dispatch*. Reprinted with permission.

The parallel message to comprehensive sex education would be: "We wish you wouldn't smoke, but if you do, smoke filtered cigarettes . . . and we will provide them to you without telling your parents."

The comprehensive safe-sex education message is also known as the "dual message." It sends adolescents a compromised and confused signal. Further, the "abstinence" component within comprehensive safe-sex programs is treated as just an alternative method to avoid pregnancy and STDs. The comprehensive safe-sex education message ignores basic human nature—that when given the option between two alternatives, some people will choose the worst alternative.

Abstinence-centered sex education, on the other hand, focuses on the root issue by seeking to reduce adolescent sexual activity rather than inadequately attempting to deal with the consequences after the fact. It treats abstinence as the healthy lifestyle choice—not just another option.

The "Fear-Based" Label

• *Isn't it true that abstinence education is "fear-based"?* With one million pregnancies and three million cases of STDs among teens per year, it is a shame that the debate on sexuality education has been reduced to name-calling.

There are two major problems with dismissing abstinence programs as "fear-based." The first problem deals with defining the terms we use. What exactly does it mean to be fear-based? Is a program fear-based if it discloses the social and economic costs of adolescent pregnancy? Is a program fear-based if it discusses the failure rates of condoms to prevent pregnancy? Is a program fear-based if it truthfully tells teens that condoms provide little or no protection against certain STDs?

Or, is a program fear-based if it simply presents an opposing viewpoint about teen sexuality? A case in point is the slide presentation produced by the Medical Institute for Sexual Health (MISH). The Sexuality Information and Education Council of the United States (SIECUS) labels the MISH material as fear-based. Yet MISH's statistics come directly from the Centers for Disease Control, the National Institute for Health, established peer-reviewed medical journals and other reputable sources of medical information.

The second problem with the fear-based label is that it assumes there is never a place for legitimate fear. In truth, entire generations of Americans have avoided various risky behaviors because of the fear of the consequences. Further, Douglas Kirby in the booklet "No Easy Answers" states that "the fear of AIDS may generate greater receptivity to information about prevention." If conveying truth about the medical, economic and social consequences of sexual promiscuity creates fear in adolescents, then perhaps a little more fear is what we need. Fear is a healthy respect for the consequences of bad decisions.

Dishonest Research

• *Didn't a recent study show that most parents are against abstinence education?* Again, the misinformation campaign is hard at work. The Durex Condom Company conducted a telephone survey that asked the following loaded question: "Do you support schools in your district accepting state and federal funds that would prevent them from teaching your children the complete facts about birth control and sexually transmitted diseases?"

Here is how Durex spun the results: "More than 82 percent responded that they do not support schools that accept abstinence-only funding."

This is not honest research. Durex knows that abstinence programs teach the complete facts about birth control and STDs. They just don't promote condoms. The question Durex asked and the results they reported have nothing to do with each other. What if Durex would have asked this question:

> Do you support schools in your district accepting federal and state funds that would mandate the promotion of condoms for unmarried teens but prevent schools from teaching your children the complete facts about the failure rates of condoms in protecting against pregnancy and certain STDs?

Is it any wonder that Durex received a sanction from both the Federal Trade Commission and the National Institute of Child Health and Human Development in 1997 for failure to meet minimum quality standards and unsubstantiated and deceptive claims about their condoms?

The TRUTH is that most parents approve of abstinence education. A major survey of 28,000 adults taken by *USA Today* in 1997 found that 56 percent thought the best way to reduce pregnancy is to teach abstinence while only 31 percent thought that the best way is to promote safe sex.

Speaking of surveys, the National Coalition for Abstinence Education (NCAE) would like to ask the readers of this viewpoint the following question right now: As parents, would you want your elected representatives in Washington, your community leaders, your school board members, your governor and your state health department officials to determine policies impacting the health of your children based on information, opinions or pressure they receive from the Durex Condom Company or Durex spokesperson Jane Fonda?

• *Isn't there research to show that abstinence programs don't work?* As the old adage goes, "figures can lie, and liars can figure." Opponents of abstinence education can find or interpret research to support anything they want to say. An example of this is the analysis of an "abstinence" program entitled ENABL (Education Now and Babies Later) in California. Abstinence-until-marriage advocates had reservations about the program from its inception, because they felt it contained some mixed messages for teens. Abstinence-plus (contraceptive) advocates supported the program—until evaluation of ENABL came out showing inconclusive results. At this point, the safe-sex education advocates distanced themselves from the program and declared abstinence education a failure.

There are credible studies to prove that abstinence programs work. But true abstinence programs, on the whole, have received little or no federal funding for research. Congress realized this situation, which is why Title V funding hopes to gather credible data on abstinence-until-marriage education programs. The REAL question is: will abstinence opponents on many state committees try to sabotage the evaluation process as they have done with the intent of the law?

Faulty Assumptions About Abstinence Education

• *What about adolescents who, for whatever reason, can't remain abstinent? Isn't it irresponsible to withhold from these teens important information which could save their lives?* This is the biggest charge against abstinence education by its opponents. And this charge is so loaded with faulty assumptions that we must address it point-by-point.

First, this question implies that abstinence education is all adolescents will receive. *This is just plain false.* We have already established in this viewpoint that funding for the safe-sex message remains intact. It is doubtful that a single student will lose access to the contraceptive message directly due to the Title V abstinence funding.

Second, this question implies that abstinence education will not discuss contraceptives, pregnancy and STDs. Wrong again. The fact is that the Title V funding cannot be used to promote contraceptive use to teens for sex outside of marriage. Abstinence programs do address contraceptives and STDs, but they do so honestly by showing the failure rates for pregnancy and disease prevention.

Third, this question implies that condoms are the answer to pregnancies and STDs. Wrong again. Study after study shows that adolescents do not use condoms correctly 100 percent of the time. The Centers for Disease Control states that "consistently means using a condom every time you have sex—100 percent of the time—no exceptions." CDC adds that "used inconsistently, condoms offer little more protection than when they are not used at all." This fact is important because studies show that basic knowledge of and access to condoms by adolescents have low correlation with consistent and correct use.

Fourth, condoms, even when used correctly, offer little or no protection against human papillomavirus (HPV) and only slightly better protection against chlamydia. Both are among America's fastest-spreading STDs. HPV is incurable, and both HPV and chlamydia, if untreated, can lead to serious medical consequences. In fact, genital cancer caused by HPV has claimed the lives of more females than AIDS.

Further, about 15 percent of female adolescents using condoms get pregnant during the first year of use. So much for the "98 percent effective" claim by the condom industry.

Fifth, NCAE acknowledges that some adolescents will choose to be sexually active no matter how much abstinence is taught. But the decision to be sexually active is a health decision. Such a decision is too serious to be promoted or facilitated by school teachers or anyone else who is not in a position of primary responsibility for the adolescent's health. It must be made with input from parents, the family's primary-care physician, a family counselor and the family's spiritual advisor—people who will strive to move the adolescent back toward truly healthy behavior.

Is Abstinence Reasonable?

• *With sexual maturity coming at a younger and younger age, and marriage coming at an older age, is it reasonable to expect people to remain abstinent until marriage?* Attacking the Title V Program on the basis of whether or not it is "realistic" to expect adults to remain abstinent until marriage is irrelevant for two reasons. First, the Title V Abstinence Education Program is aimed at adolescents because they are more susceptible to STDs, have a less developed and more emotionally driven decision-making capacity, are more influenced by peer pressure and make choices that reflect an attitude of invincibility.

Second, and more important, true realism demands we recognize that the sexual revolution has proven to be a disaster for American society. Congress has done just that, calling for a paradigm shift in the best medical, emotional and economic interest of America. In this it is following a distinguished precedent: Congress has taken similar bold action before in our history—for example, on drugs, racial equality and smoking. It is unfortunate that some people cannot accept the courageous act of Congress and are attempting to sabotage the law.

• *Given all of the above answers, why would someone be opposed to the Title V Abstinence Education Program?* That's a great question. Frankly, we really don't understand how someone can intellectually oppose the clear message that sexual abstinence among adolescents is the best choice for their physical, emotional, educational and economic future.

But we do know that an entire industry exists in the U.S. because children are getting pregnant and contracting STDs. This industry would be financially harmed if adolescents should turn toward abstinence.

The safe-sex advocates (SIECUS, Planned Parenthood, Jane Fonda, Durex and their ideological allies) have held a monopoly on sexuality education since 1971. During their reign, adolescent pregnancies and STDs have reached epidemic levels.

As a society, we can argue forever about the details of this study or that study or this research or that research. But the reality is that teen pregnancies and STDs have skyrocketed during a time when comprehensive safe-sex education has been the dominant message in America's classrooms. And on this basis alone, the safe-sex message must be considered a world-class failure.

Congress realized this, which is why it passed a bold, visionary and unapologetic new law.

The abstinence message deserves a fair, full and uncompromised chance. It's the least we can do for our children.

"We teach children how to have sex with someone else. Why not discuss how to have sex with themselves?"

Students Should Be Taught About Masturbation

Mary Renee Smith

Sex education should include information about masturbation, argues Mary Renee Smith in the following viewpoint. Schoolchildren should learn that self-gratification is a normal and acceptable type of sexual behavior, she contends. Since students are instructed about intercourse, condoms, and STDs, they should also be taught that masturbation is a commonly practiced, no-risk sexual activity. Smith is a journalism and mass communications student at Kansas State University in Manhattan, Kansas.

As you read, consider the following questions:

1. What are some of the past myths about masturbation, according to Smith?
2. What is the main reason that people have sex, in the author's opinion?
3. According to Smith, why was Joycelyn Elders fired from her position as Surgeon General?

Reprinted from "Sex Education Lacking One Important Part," by Mary Renee Smith, online publication of Student Publications, Inc., Kansas State University, January 22, 1996, at www.spub.ksu.edu/issues/v100/SP/n076/opn-smith.html.

You can have unprotected sex with someone you know very well, someone who knows exactly what you like and how you like it, with no risk of pregnancy or any other terminal side effects.

This person won't think you are kinky, loud or looking for commitment.

It's that thing you never talk about, but Beavis and Butt-Head can make into a half-hour show. Masturbation.

Everybody Does It

There are so many more creative phrases for the art of masturbation, but I'll leave those in your hands.

Everybody does it. Some of you have done it today. Some of you will do it later. And some of you could be doing it right now. Not a pretty picture, I must admit.

It amazes me through all the years of sex education lectures, films and cheesy public service announcements, I don't remember ever being told anything about masturbation.

I know at first it seems a strange concept—including masturbation in sex education. Why not? We teach children how to have sex with someone else. Why not discuss how to have sex with themselves?

Sex education should begin at home. But personally, I cannot imagine my mother discussing masturbation. This woman's idea of a birth control pill was putting an aspirin between your knees and holding it there.

She convinced my sister that eating chocolate makes your body release the same hormones and produce the same euphoria as having sex.

My sister's running joke is "Snickers—the bar that really satisfies."

The church didn't offer much more guidance. I was taught you only touch yourself for the two W's, wiping and washing. Even then, if it took more than two seconds, you had to go to confession.

Myths About Masturbation

Of course, if you can't scare the public with morality, you can convince them what they are doing will make them sick.

The myths began long ago. Hairy palms, bad eyesight,

poor hearing.

During the 1700s, doctors said the nervous system could be damaged by the convulsive effects of orgasm. If you're happy, and you know it—twitch your head!

If the urge to masturbate gets too strong, you might try a bowl of cornflakes. During the 1800s, J.H. Kellogg wrote a popular book that suggested a diet including cornflakes to stifle those evil desires.

He listed some tell-tale signs of a masturbator. See how many of your friends have these symptoms: rounded shoulders, weak backs, paleness, acne, bashfulness, boldness and confusion.

The Safest Sex Around

Home and school, in that order, remain the ideal settings in which to inform kids about sexuality. So why not include masturbation in the just-say-no curriculum so many parents and teachers adore? After all, it's not about "how to" and "try this," it's about options: reminding kids of a safe way to cope with increasing sexual desires without jumping into bed with someone. Perhaps the message simply needs to be modified to "just say yes to sex with yourself, and no to anyone else who happens to come along." Masturbation is, after all, the safest sex around.

Denise Kiernan, *Village Voice*, January 21, 1997.

These touchers-of-themselves may also mock piety, bite their nails or wet the bed.

Kellogg claimed masturbators were more likely to start using tobacco. And you thought nicotine addiction was how the tobacco industry hooked you. Now you know why Joe the Camel has those sexy humps.

Pleasure Should Be Acceptable

Talking about masturbation makes more sense than the myths, silence and giggles the subject now brings up.

If we knew how to please ourselves, we would not be so anxious to have sex with someone else. Sex with someone else would be better if we knew what pleased us to begin with.

Let's be honest. We are not having sex to reproduce. We

are having sex because it feels good. Occasionally incredible.

For a few moments in time you believe in Santa Claus and the real possibility of world peace. There is no shame in that. Pleasure is a very powerful force.

But alas, masturbation is a dirty word and is better left alone. Joycelyn Elders was fired from being Surgeon General in 1994 for even suggesting we include masturbation in our sex education programs.

Teach kids about disease and condom use, but heaven forbid we tell them they can please themselves at no risk to anyone.

It always amazes me that everything about sex has to be labeled moral or immoral, right or wrong. If you do something that feels good and doesn't hurt anyone, no one should care.

Masturbation is the one form of sex we all have in common. Let's have Masturbation Pride Day. With a parade and T-shirts, even.

It could be day when everyone admits they like pleasure and it's OK. Everyone does it, everyone knows everyone does it, and no one cares.

Interesting concept, sexuality without judgment.

> "The crude, loveless, sexually promiscuous world we have created for our kids is not unrelated to teaching them a hydraulic view of sex."

Students Should Not Be Taught About Masturbation

Mona Charen

Sex education programs should not promote masturbation, argues syndicated columnist Mona Charen in the following viewpoint. Educators who advocate instruction about masturbation subscribe to the "hydraulic view" of sex—the idea that sexual urges must find release because they are too powerful to resist. Emphasizing masturbation as a "safe" form of gratification, Charen contends, denies the fact that teenagers are moral beings who have the ability to delay sexual activity until they are in a mature, committed relationship.

As you read, consider the following questions:
1. Which major publications defended Joycelyn Elders's proposal to teach masturbation in the schools, according to Charen?
2. Those who promote education about masturbation base their arguments on what two assumptions, in the author's opinion?
3. How have liberal sex educators damaged relationships between male and female teenagers, in Charen's view?

Reprinted from "Some Things Best Left in Closet," by Mona Charen, *Denver Rocky Mountain News*, December 22, 1994, by permission of Mona Charen and Creators Syndicate.

There's a prayer that goes "Oh Lord, let my enemies go too far" that comes to mind when one considers former Surgeon General Joycelyn Elders and her advocates.

She does have advocates, it turns out, even if President Bill Clinton offered the unconvincing explanation that her statements were at variance with his "values." At first blush, Elders' remarks about teaching masturbation in the schools seemed, in the words of Kay Hymowitz of the Manhattan Institute, to be a hilarious instance of "bringing coals to Newcastle."

Must Masturbation Be Highlighted?

But the humorless liberals at the *New York Times* and *Washington Post* were hot to defend Elders and her proposal. The *Times* ran a scolding story about masturbation myths through the centuries, titled "America Keeps Onan in the Closet," in which Charles Dickens, Sylvester Graham (of the crackers) and J.H. Kellogg (corn flakes) all come in for their share of shame for propagating myths about the consequences of masturbation.

Hasn't the poor American closet been emptied enough? Must masturbation now make its debut in the spotlight? Will we be condemned to listen to the public confessions of those who used to feel shame about the practice but now wish to go public?

What good is supposed to come of this? The answer, from Elders and from Frank Rich of the *New York Times* and Patrick Welsh writing in the *Washington Post*, is fewer unplanned pregnancies. The *Post* calls masturbation "the safest sex." And the *New York Times* calls it "The Last Taboo" (don't bet on it).

If they are right, we have to assume a few facts. The first is that masturbation is inadequately understood by youngsters. But the second, and more serious, point is this: Trust in sex education, condom distribution and the rest is founded on an idea—I call it the hydraulic view of sex—and if you believe in that idea, then teaching masturbation is no more peculiar than teaching "safe sex."

The hydraulic view of sex amounts to the belief that sexual orgasm is a physical release, like exhaling. Pressure builds in the adolescent body, goes the reasoning, and it must find release. It is foolish to tell children not to indulge in sexual behavior because the pressures are too great to resist. Sex educators, like Elders, are accordingly enthusiastic about every method for keeping kids from suffering the consequences of their behavior.

Welsh describes young people "without the imagination to masturbate." Willing sex partners are so plentiful, he explains, that masturbation is unnecessary. He then goes on to lament the lack of courtship among teen-agers. "According to several family-life teachers, the old concept of working one's way to first base in boy-girl relationships is not in the game plan for many kids."

What the masturbation enthusiasts can't see is that the crude, loveless, sexually promiscuous world we have created for kids is not unrelated to teaching them a hydraulic view of sex. Sure, the culture sends the wrong messages. But so do sex education programs that speak in terms of "skills" and methods and condoms.

"... And now, class, a moment of silent prayer before we begin our masturbation lesson."

Jim Borgman. Reprinted by special permission of King Features Syndicate.

What a difference it would make if sex educators took the view that teen-agers are moral actors, fully human personalities with a spiritual dimension, instead of tightly wound bundles of hormones. Wouldn't it be revolutionary to speak of love and commitment in connection with sex? And wouldn't it be brave to assume that our teen-agers are capable of delaying gratification, as millions of their forebears have done?

The liberal regime in sexual matters has bequeathed our kids a world in which raw appetite alone governs sex. Girls get little respect from the boys to whom they submit, and boys learn nothing of the ancient art of courtship. Leave it to Elders and Co. to conclude that the answer is instruction in masturbation.

"*Children are already learning about [sexual orientation in public schools]. The problem is they are often receiving inaccurate, destructive messages.*"

Schools Should Teach Students About Homosexuality

Beth Reis

In the following viewpoint, Beth Reis argues that educators should counteract damaging antigay stereotypes by taking an active and positive role in teaching about sexual orientation. Gay, lesbian, bisexual, transgendered, and straight students all need to receive accurate and constructive information about same-sex attraction and sexual identity, maintains Reis. Prejudice and ignorance about sexual minorities must be replaced by a respectful awareness about sexual orientation—particularly since schools and society are witnessing an increase in violence against homosexuals. Reis is a public health educator affiliated with the Safe Schools Coalition of Washington in Seattle.

As you read, consider the following questions:
1. According to Reis, what percentage of Americans are homosexual or bisexual?
2. What do some youths do in an attempt to prove their maleness or femaleness, according to the author?
3. What information does Reis offer to counteract the myth that homosexual relationships do not last?

Excerpted from "A Guide to Teaching Actively About Sexual Orientation" and "Important Points to Make to Students When Discussing Sexual Orientation," by Beth Reis, *SIECUS Report*, April/May 1998. Reprinted with permission.

W e really don't have a choice when it comes to teaching about sexual orientation in public schools. Children are already learning about it. The problem is they are often receiving inaccurate, destructive messages.

Author Katherine Whitlock said in her book *Bridges of Respect: Creating Support for Gay and Lesbian Youth* that:

> In schools across the country, even very young children learn the codes, passed on in jokes and whispers: "Don't wear certain colors to school on a particular day, or you're queer." Lessons are learned each time a child discovers that one of the surest ways to deliver an insult is to accuse another of being a *lezzy*, a *faggot*, a *sissy*. Children may not always know what these words mean, but they know the pejorative power of this language. Lessons are learned each time adults speak and act as if everyone in the world is heterosexual, or should be. Adult acquiescence in homophobia places lesbian and gay youth at great emotional and sometimes physical risk.

All students, regardless of their sexual orientation, learn mythology and hatred in school. All are hurt by it. Teachers can educate *actively*, replacing mythology with knowledge and hatred with respect, or they can educate *passively* as they have in the past. Those are the only alternatives. Either way, they communicate important messages.

Teaching Actively

There are a number of important reasons why teachers should teach *actively:*

• *Because it is personally important to many children.* Between 2 and 9 percent of Americans are homosexual or bisexual. This means a high school with a student body of 1,000 probably has 20 to 90 gay, lesbian, and bisexual students (plus a few who are transgender). In addition, some students also have a brother, sister, mother, or father who is a sexual minority. At least six million children in the United States have a gay or lesbian parent. Every child deserves accurate information and respectful messages about himself or herself or about loved ones.

• *Because it can build self-esteem and resiliency.* Teachers need to tell gay, lesbian, and bisexual youth that they are good people and that they have faith in them. This would help reduce the likelihood that they will, as a disproportionate number of sexual minority youth do, engage in such self-destructive behaviors as dropping out of school, abusing alcohol and other drugs, becoming homeless (by choice or not), experiencing sexual abuse and exploitation, or considering suicide.

• *Because it can help support and enhance relationships in all families.* Sexual minority youth are sometimes embraced and cherished by their families. More often, however, they fear rejection and hide their feelings from their families. Teachers can provide information to parents and put them in touch with other parents. They can help some students to feel confident and strong enough to confide in their families.

Not all families, of course, can accept their gay and lesbian children. Some teens who come out to their families are assaulted and/or kicked out of their homes. One study found that 8 percent of gay and 11 percent of lesbian youth were physically abused by parents or siblings because of their sexual orientation. In Seattle, 40 percent of homeless youth are gay, lesbian, or bisexual. Teachers can provide supportive resources for these youth. They can also help heterosexual students become allies for family members who are gay, lesbian, or bisexual.

Counteracting Prejudice and Violence

• *Because it can counteract stereotypes and prejudice as well as reduce the likelihood of violence.* In the poignant words of one seventh grader, "God made all of us so we're all special in our own way. So stop the names because if you don't think I'm special, you're wrong. . . ."

The U.S. Department of Justice reports that homosexuals are probably the most frequent victims of hate-motivated violence in the nation. Schools are actually one of the least safe places for openly gay and gender role nonconforming youth and for those who voice support for gay and lesbian civil rights. Students are sometimes publicly humiliated, threatened, chased, followed, spit on, assaulted, and raped.

Gay, lesbian, and bisexual youth who witness harassment of gay peers often react by hiding their orientation even more vigorously out of fear or self-hate. Some protect themselves by joining in the bullying. Heterosexuals who observe the persecution may experience guilt about their silent complicity and a sense of powerlessness similar to that experienced by their homosexual, bisexual, and transgendered peers.

Students learn early on to rigidly comply with gender roles. Students fear becoming targets of harassment . . . regardless of their sexual orientation. Young men may have sexual relations with girls as a way of proving their maleness. Similarly, young women may get pregnant to try to prove their femaleness. . . .

The Need for Accurate Information

Only accurate information can replace the ignorance and stereotypes that hurt all children. These are points which teachers will want to consider making when discussing sexual orientation with their students:

• *A same-sex crush, dream, or relationship is not necessarily gay or lesbian.* Students need to know that many adults who identify as heterosexual report some homosexual experiences. They also need to know that many homosexual adults report having had heterosexual experiences. Thus, a single experience has no predictive value. Students must be helped not to label themselves prematurely. On the other hand, adults must understand that not all such youth are "just going through a phase." Many may have already realized that they are much more attracted to people of their own gender. More than a few gay men and lesbians say they sensed something "different" about themselves as early as four or five years of age. Most young gay men acknowledge their sexual orientation between 14 and 16 years of age while most young lesbians acknowledge their sexual orientation between 16 and 19 years of age. To dismiss students' feelings is to dismiss a core part of their personalities. It can deprive them of the opportunity to support their quest for integrity and maturity.

• *Gay, lesbian, bisexual, and transgendered youth sometimes believe they can change by dating a person of the other sex or by marrying and having children.* These youth need to understand that there are no scientifically valid studies that indicate people can change their sexual orientation or identity. Even therapy or religious experiences apparently cannot eliminate these feelings although some studies have documented limited success at extinguishing same-sex behavior in highly motivated bisexual individuals. They need to know that many gays and lesbians are happy with their orientation and do not want to change.

Gay Adolescents Lack Support

• A 1988 national survey of heterosexual male youths 15 to 19 years old found that only 12 percent felt that they could have a gay person as a friend.

• In a 14-city survey, nearly three-fourths of lesbian and gay youth first disclosed their sexual identity to friends: 46 percent lost a friend after coming out to her or him.

• Less than one in five gay and lesbian adolescent students surveyed could identify someone who was very supportive of them.

SIECUS Report, April/May 1998.

• *The classmates of children with gay or lesbian parents sometimes mistakenly conclude that they, too, are homosexual.* They need to know that the sexual orientation of parents does not determine the sexual orientation of the child. Youth who grow up in gay or lesbian households may have a better appreciation of diversity or be more skilled at coping with prejudice. They are as likely as other youth to be heterosexual.

Other Myths About Sexual Orientation

• *Gay and lesbian youth often mistakenly believe the stereotypes that all gay men are effeminate and that all lesbian women are masculine.* As a result, they may experience cognitive dissonance. To resolve it, they may adopt new stereotyped personas which only increase their sense of alienation from self, family, and peers. Others attempt to rigidly deny their same-sex feelings and compulsively invest their energy in becoming the perfect student, the perfect son or daughter, the perfect athlete. This perfectionism often leads to defeat and self-destructive behavior. In reality, homosexual people are as diverse in their dress, their behavior, and their choice of occupations as heterosexual people.

• *Children who are sexually abused may mistakenly assume it has made them gay or lesbian, especially if the exploitative same-sex touch involved any physical pleasure.* Part of the reason that sexual abuse is so confusing to young people is that it sometimes evokes a pleasurable physical response while also evoking fear, humiliation, and hurt. Students must learn that bodies do sometimes respond that way and that means neither that the victim consented nor that she or he was wrong. Young people need to know that there is no evidence that sexual trauma influences sexual orientation.

• *Gay and lesbian youth often believe the myth that homosexual relationships don't last.* Students need to understand that there are long-term, committed same-sex relationships. One study found that 71 percent of gay men live with a partner. Another found that 82 percent of lesbians live with a partner. According to researchers from the University of Washington, "couplehood," either as a reality or an aspiration, is as strong among gay people as among heterosexuals . . . even though there is much less social and institutional support for permanence and commitment.

• *Heterosexual youth often believe that only gay men get AIDS.* This leads to a very dangerous false confidence. A teen who considers himself or herself heterosexual may feel no need to abstain from sexual relations or from protection while having sexual relations. Students need to understand that it is their *behavior,* not their *sexual orientation* that puts them at risk. HIV can infect anyone (male or female; homosexual, bisexual, or heterosexual; married or single) who has unprotected sexual relations with, or shares a needle with a person who is infected with HIV.

Fears Associated with Homosexuality

• *Children with a gay or lesbian parent may unnecessarily fear that all homosexuals will contract HIV and get AIDS.* Again, *behavior* (not *sexual orientation*) puts an individual at risk. Children who love someone gay or lesbian need to understand this. How sad for a young person to live with the fear that they will lose their parent (sibling, grandparent, aunt, or uncle) to AIDS . . . especially when that loved one may actually be at less risk than the general public because they practice safe behaviors.

• *Sexual minority teens may avoid seeking health services or reporting physical or sexual assaults to school authorities or police for fear of unprofessional treatment.* Young people may lose their lives to AIDS or to "gay bashers" when they harbor the unfortunate stereotype of adults, when they fear discrimination, or when they don't trust that their confidentiality will be maintained by the professionals they approach. Teachers can't assure teens that these things won't happen. They need to acknowledge that these fears exist. They also need to help students recognize the importance of seeking help when they are in crisis. They can help students understand that some doctors, police, parents, teachers, and counselors are sensitive, respectful, and trustworthy.

> "*[The] federal government will
> eventually criminalize opposition of
> any kind to homosexuality—and
> American schoolchildren are being
> prepared for that very day.*"

Schools Should Not Teach Students to Accept Homosexuality

William Norman Grigg

There has been a harmful proliferation of homosexual-rights propaganda in the nation's schools, maintains William Norman Grigg in the following viewpoint. Students are being taught that the pro-gay attitude is the only "correct" stance on homosexuality despite the fact that many parents do not support the homosexual rights agenda. In Grigg's opinion, homosexuality is a dangerous vice that can lead to disease, sexual addiction, and self-destruction. Grigg is a senior editor for the *New American*, a biweekly journal published by the John Birch Society.

As you read, consider the following questions:
1. In Grigg's opinion, what is ironic about the Clinton Administration's position on teen smoking in comparison to its stance on homosexuality?
2. According to the author, what happened during the 1998 event co-hosted by the Human Rights Campaign at the University of California at Santa Cruz?
3. According to Grigg, what conclusions about homosexuality are drawn in the video *It's Elementary: Talking About Gay Issues in School*?

Excerpted from "They Want Your Children," by William Norman Grigg, *The New American*, June 8, 1998. Reprinted with permission.

Homosexuality is a chosen behavior with self-destructive consequences. Young people sometimes fall prey to it in early adolescence; the initial repugnance provoked by the vice in many cases yields to fascination and eventually results in addiction. As a result of homosexuality, promising lives are cut tragically short by disease, and health care costs are incurred that are absorbed by families and the community at large.

Every element of this description applies to smoking, a practice that, unlike homosexuality, is not condemned by the Bible as an abomination before God and has not been denounced by millennia of Western moral teaching as a dire perversion. Just as there are many people who have abandoned tobacco after adolescent experimentation or even years of regular use, there are many people who have abandoned the vice of homosexuality after dabbling with it as confused adolescents or struggling with it for years. Accordingly, the contrast between the Clinton Administration's crusade against youth smoking and its efforts to encourage acceptance of homosexual behavior among youth is instructive.

Dangerous Double Standard

"Today, the epidemic of teen smoking is raging throughout our nation as, one by one, our children are lured by multimillion dollar marketing schemes designed to do exactly that," intoned Mr. Bill Clinton in a March 7, 1998, radio address. "Three thousand children start to smoke every day illegally, and 1,000 of them will die sooner because of it. This is a national tragedy that every American should be honorbound to prevent."

After enumerating the steps already taken to "educate" schoolchildren about the evils of tobacco, "reduce their access to tobacco products," and severely "restrict tobacco companies from advertising to young people," Mr. Clinton insisted that "even this is not enough to fully protect our children." He urged the public to support legislation that would dramatically raise the price of cigarettes, penalize the tobacco industry if it "keeps selling cigarettes to our children," and "restrict tobacco ads aimed at young people, so that our children can't fall prey to the deadly threat of tobacco."

In short, the Clinton Administration, in defiance of constitutional impediments, seeks to mobilize the full regulatory and enforcement resources of the central government in a campaign to protect schoolchildren against a form of self-destructive behavior. Of course, no similar crusade has been mounted by the Administration to discourage the similarly self-destructive form of behavior called homosexuality.

For anti-tobacco zealots, the evil lure of tobacco is embodied in "Joe Camel," a commercial mascot created by R.J. Reynolds Company whose seductive appeal supposedly overpowers the resistance of suggestible youth. Teen smoking, claimed Bill Clinton recently, "has everything to do with Joe Camel." In her syndicated newspaper column, Hillary Clinton inveighed against actress Julia Roberts for chain-smoking in the popular film *My Best Friend's Wedding*. "Movie stars who puff away on screen equate smoking with status, power, confidence, and glamour," pontificated Mrs. Clinton. The First Lady did not condemn the same film for featuring a homosexual character that embodied "status, power, confidence, and glamour," of course.

Propagandizing on Behalf of Homosexuality

Thus, it is not surprising that the same Clinton Administration which has made Joe Camel a totem of evil has embraced homosexual actress Ellen DeGeneres, who has made herself a living advertisement for the normalization of her chosen perversion. DeGeneres and her "lover" Anne Heche have been welcomed at White House social events, and have been photographed with the President.

In an October 16, 1997, speech before the Hollywood Radio and Television Society, Vice President Al Gore applauded DeGeneres for using her television program to propagandize on behalf of homosexuality. When she "came out" on her program, Gore explained to a Hollywood audience, "millions of Americans were forced to look at sexual orientation in a more open light." Compounding the irony is the fact that DeGeneres, in a fit of petulant militancy, demanded that the ABC television network remove the "TV 14" rating from her program, in order to make it more accessible to impressionable children.

The Administration's anti-tobacco rhetoric casts tobacco

companies as predators who brazenly target young potential customers as a means of expanding their markets. Whether or not this charge applies to tobacco companies, it is certainly true of radical homosexual activists. Writing in *The Advocate*, lesbian activist Donna Minkowitz urged her comrades to "take the offensive for a change, whether the issue is promiscuity or recruiting the previously straight. . . . Ten percent is not enough! Recruit, recruit, recruit!"

Blatant Manipulation

If some of the teachers do not explicitly say that people are wrong when they oppose homosexuality, they do so implicitly. The words "gays and lesbians" are circled on the chalkboard in the third-grade class of teacher Daithi Wolfe, at Hawthorne Elementary School in Madison, Wisconsin. Then, as he begins to write down the words that students associate with homosexuality, a curious pattern develops. Any negative words offered by students about homosexuals are placed on the right side of his circle: "Homophobia." "Discrimination." "Name-calling." "Weird." And, of course, "Nazis" and "Hitler."

But on the left side of the board—apparently the side with the "right" words—are "pink triangle," "rainbow necklace," "same (as real people)," and "equal rights." Such blatant manipulation might not work on adults, but it is clearly effective on children.

Ed Vitagliano, *AFA Journal*, June 1997.

The July 15, 1993, *Washington Post* reported that recruiting efforts are enjoying success. In many Washington, DC-area public schools, noted the *Post*, students are not only discussing "gay rights" issues in class, but also "declaring their own bisexuality or homosexuality, a step some said they were taking to be trendy or cool." Some students, in fact, "outed" themselves merely "to protect themselves from just being normal."

If evidence were to emerge that a tobacco company had targeted schoolchildren as "closeted" smokers, and had insinuated propaganda into public school classrooms to encourage them to "experiment" with tobacco, the ATF and FDA would probably mount a paramilitary raid on the company's corporate offices and drag its executives off to jail in leg irons. Yet the Clinton Administration has energetically supported efforts to normalize homosexuality and to compel social acceptance of the vice, and those efforts are carried out in many of the same public school classrooms in which schoolchildren are catechized about the evils of smoking.

Reality Behind the Rhetoric

Early in Bill Clinton's first term, Andrew Kopkind of *The Nation* magazine pointed out that "homosexuality is—by presidential directive—a positive qualification for an Administration job." Mr. Clinton retains his penchant for the pervert lobby.

In November 1997, Bill Clinton convened a summit on "hate crimes" at the White House, an event to which radical homosexual activists were conspicuously invited. In remarks at that event, Mr. Clinton declared, "Children have to be taught to hate. We need to make sure someone is teaching them not to do so." In the vocabulary of the left, "hatred" includes rejection of homosexuality and opposition to the political demands of the Lavender Lobby. The largest and most high-profile of the radical homosexual groups involved in the fight against "hatred" is the Human Rights Campaign (HRC), which hosted President Clinton at a fundraising dinner in Washington, DC, in 1998.

A few weeks after President Clinton conferred his imprimatur on the HRC, the group co-hosted an event at the University of California–Santa Cruz entitled "Exposed!" The four-day event, which drew high school and college students, as well as educators and activists, was a festival of hard-core pornography and radical activism. Workshops included a lecture by prostitute Teresa Dulce and a performance by "pleasure activist" Annie Sprinkle which included excerpts from her X-rated videos. Another film offering at the event was entitled *Blood Sisters: Leather Dykes & Sado-masochism and Daddy at the Muscle Academy*. . . .

Teaching Tools

In 1996, the National Education Association (NEA)—which was arguably the most powerful element of the Clinton coalition—adopted as part of its bylaws Resolution B-7, which deals with "Racism, Sexism, and Sexual Orientation Discrimination." The measure called for the elimination of "discrimination" against homosexuality, the imposition of policies to "increase acceptance" of "gays and lesbians," the integration of an "accurate portrayal" of homosexuals "throughout history and across the curriculum," the eradication of "subtle practices that favor the education of one student over another on the basis of . . . sexual orientation," and the development and implementation of "training programs on these matters."

One of the tools available to achieve the goals outlined by the NEA is a video entitled *It's Elementary: Talking About Gay Issues in School*, which has been screened in classrooms across the country. Set in six elementary and middle schools, the agit-prop video depicts supposedly candid discussions between "enlightened" teachers and schoolchildren. The discussions follow a predictable script: Homosexuals are treated as oppressed victims; objection to the practice is scorned as bigotry; and Christianity is singled out for individualized condemnation.

"Some Christians believe if you're gay, you'll go to hell, so they want to torture them and stuff like that," insists a fifth grader with the enthusiastic certainty typical of misled innocence. An eighth grader recites one of the sodomite lobby's preferred sophistries: "If kids are too young to be taught about homosexuality, then they are too young to be taught about heterosexuality." A first-grade teacher from Wisconsin insists that parents should be compelled to enroll their children in sodomite mind-laundry classes: "If parents are allowed to have their children opt out of gay and lesbian units [classes], what will happen when we teach about Dutch culture or African-American history? It scares me."

"*It's Elementary* is the latest tool in a fast-growing campaign," reports Robert H. Knight of the Family Research Council. "A homosexual teachers group, Gay, Lesbian and Straight Teachers Network (GLSTN), has produced its own video, *Teaching Respect for All*, as part of its second annual 'back to school' campaign. The 50-minute video is based on the staff training program created by GLSTN for the Massachusetts Department of Education under Republican Governor William Weld.". . .

The Gains of the Sodomite Revolution

Newsweek for November 8, 1993, reported that in Massachusetts, "National Coming Out Day" is "an autumnal rite every bit as gala as graduation day. . . ." In the state that contributed homosexual Congressman Barney Frank to the House of Representatives, noted *Newsweek*, "multiculturalism has come to embrace multisexualism." Thus "more students seem to be coming out, and they're coming out younger. A climate of greater tolerance is making it possible for teens to explore more openly what they've historically sampled in secret."

One of those responsible for the expanding epidemic among Massachusetts teenagers is Karen Harbeck of the Massachusetts Governor's Advisory Commission on Gay and Lesbian Youth. Speaking in June 1997 at the Second Congress on Family Law and the Rights of Children in San Francisco, Harbeck proudly outlined the gains made by the sodomite revolution: "Ten years ago, the average age of 'coming out of the closet' for gay men was 26; the average age for lesbians was 28. On the average, young people today are coming out of the closet at age 15. . . . And if you come out of the closet at age 14, 15, or 16, you've probably been gay or lesbian for the previous six years and had no one to talk to."

While most people would be startled by the idea of a "closeted" eight-year-old, Harbeck insists that public schools have to "liberate" such children—now designated as "Gay, Lesbian, Bisexual, Trans-sexual, or Questioning" (GLBTQ) youth—at the earliest possible age. "By seventh grade it's too late," Harbeck insisted. "People say this is an issue mainly for high school sex education class. They're wrong; it belongs in pre-school."

"Gay Pride" in School?

One result of the "gay youth" revolution in Massachusetts, observes LaBarbera, "has been a proliferation of horror stories, as parents get wind of one-sided, pro-homosexual 'lessons' or even 'gay pride' rallies at their child's school, often after the fact." Typical of this trend is the case of Mike Chiusano of Beverly, Massachusetts, who in 1994 was denounced as a "homophobe" at the dinner table by his then-14-year-old daughter after she had attended four days of mandatory assemblies entitled "Homophobia Week." "When Mr. Chiusano protested to the Beverly High administrators, his family became the victim of a harassment campaign, including a phone call to his wife from one zealot who threatened, 'We know where your daughter lives,'" recalls LaBarbera.

In March 1997, Douglas Matthews, the faculty adviser to the "gay-straight alliance" at Algonquin Regional High School, distributed a "Questionnaire about Heterosexuality" to students in a freshman history class. The questionnaire was designed to expose and rebuke "homophobic" attitudes among students. Among the questions contained in the handout was the following: "If you've never slept with a person of the same sex and enjoyed it, is it possible that all you need is a good gay lover?"

A similar document was distributed to students at Cupertino High School in California. Entitled "Heterosexuality: Can It be Cured?" the leaflet, distributed by the American Public Health Association Caucus of Gay and Public Health Workers, declared: "Heterosexuality is a condition characterized by a sexual attraction to members of the opposite gender. Many persons, in all cultures, at all times, have been heterosexual. . . . Whatever the cause of this phenomenon, we can state without doubt that there are many problems associated with heterosexuality, both for the individual and society at large." Among the "problems" listed were pregnancy and "a state of homophobia." Suggested "cures" for heterosexuality included psychotherapy and widespread sterilization of the heterosexual population.

The time is not far distant when it may be a federal offense for anyone in either the public or the private sectors to present smoking in a positive—or even neutral—context. If present trends in the classroom are any guide, the same federal government will eventually criminalize opposition of any kind to homosexuality—and American schoolchildren are being prepared for that dreadful day.

Periodical Bibliography

The following articles have been selected to supplement the diverse views presented in this chapter. Addresses are provided for periodicals not indexed in the *Readers' Guide to Periodical Literature*, the *Alternative Press Index*, the *Social Sciences Index*, or the *Index to Legal Periodicals and Books*.

Norma J. Bailey and Tracy Phariss — "Gay Students in Middle School," *Education Digest*, October 1996.

Francesca Delbanco — "No-Sex Ed," *Seventeen*, October 1997.

Education Digest — "Curricular Programs to Curb Teen Pregnancy," March 1999.

Amitai Etzioni — "Education for Intimacy," *Tikkun*, March/April 1997.

David Friedman — "Look Who's Teaching Sex," *Good Housekeeping*, November 1996.

Russell W. Gough — "Does Abstinence Education Work?" *World & I*, August 1997. Available from 3600 New York Ave. NE, Washington, DC 20002.

Tamar Lewin — "Sexual-Abstinence Grants Put to Broad Use by States," *New York Times*, April 4, 1999.

Joe S. McIlhaney Jr. and Debra W. Haffner — "Symposium: Are Abstinence-Only Sex-Education Programs Good for Teenagers?" *Insight*, September 29, 1997. Available from 3600 New York Ave. NE, Washington, DC 20002.

Richard Nadler — "Abstaining from Sex Education," *National Review*, September 9, 1997.

Kristine Napier — "Chastity Programs Shatter Sex-Ed Myths," *Policy Review*, May/June 1997.

Eric Rofes — "Gay Issues, Schools, and the Right-Wing Backlash," *Rethinking Schools*, Spring 1997.

Lynn Rosellini — "Joycelyn Elders Is Master of Her Domain," *U.S. News & World Report*, November 3, 1997.

Gary Thomas — "Where True Love Waits," *Christianity Today*, March 1, 1999.

Paul C. Vitz — "Teach Students to Value Relationships," *Education Digest*, May 1999.

Pat Wingert — "How to Talk to Kids About Sex," *Newsweek*, June 14, 1999.

CHAPTER 4

Are Some Sexual Practices Unacceptable?

Chapter Preface

Thomas Schiro was thrown out of a coin-operated "peep-show" booth because he exposed himself to a clerk. Shortly afterwards, he sexually assaulted a young woman, bludgeoned her to death, then raped her corpse and chewed on several parts of her body. Schiro claimed that he committed these crimes because he had been repeatedly exposed to violent pornography since early childhood. One expert testifying at Schiro's criminal trial stated that constant exposure to hard-core pornography creates "a person who no longer distinguishes between violence and rape, or violence and sex."

Schiro was convicted of rape and murder and therefore held fully accountable for his violent acts. However, some analysts maintain that the producers of pornography are also responsible for sexual brutality. Donna Rice Hughes, communications director of Enough Is Enough!, a women's group opposed to hard-core pornography, contends that pornographers should be held liable for provoking sexual assaults: "Ours would be a brutish society indeed if communities could not hold accountable those who incited violence and vicious crimes." Moreover, Hughes argues, even soft-core pornography cheapens sex and demoralizes society: "The best case for pornography is that some pornography is less destructive, preying on our deepest needs and diminishing our capacity for intimacy. In its most destructive forms, pornography directly contributes to sexual violence. Either way, society derives no benefit from pornography."

Nadine Strossen, author of *Defending Pornography: Free Speech, Sex, and the Fight for Women's Rights*, disputes the contention that pornography is harmful. In fact, she argues, pornography often depicts men and women in egalitarian sexual relationships, using "images and ideas that may well be seen as positive for women and feminists." Beyond its instructive and entertainment value, Strossen maintains, pornography offers a safe outlet for those who do not have sexual contact with others, including "shy or inhibited people, people with mental or physical disabilities, people with emotional problems . . . geographically isolated people, unattractive people." Pornography may even relieve people of the impulse to commit sexually violent acts, asserts Strossen. In her view, pornography should be seen as a form of free speech that can help people understand and enjoy their own sexuality.

Whether society should condone pornography, prostitution, and other alternatives to mainstream sexual standards is fiercely debated by the authors of the following chapter.

"Pornography is not ugly; our society's attitudes about sex are ugly."

Pornography Is Beneficial

Nina Hartley

Society should not be ashamed of the sexual activity that is displayed in pornography, argues Nina Hartley in the following viewpoint. In fact, she maintains, high-quality pornography is beneficial because it celebrates the pleasure of sexuality—the instinctual life force that all humans share in common. In Hartley's view, the existence of objectionable, tasteless pornography never justifies the suppression of sexually explicit images and texts. She concludes that concerned citizens should actively oppose any attempted censorship of sexually graphic materials. Hartley is an adult film actress and an activist in feminist and anticensorship issues.

As you read, consider the following questions:

1. In Hartley's opinion, what is fueling the current "anti-sex hysteria"?
2. How can pornography save civilization, in the author's view?
3. According to Hartley, why does objectionable, poor-quality pornography exist?

Reprinted, with permission, from "Pornography at the Millennium: Some Thoughts," by Nina Hartley, *Gauntlet*, vol. 2, 1997.

In trying to "come up with" a focus for this essay, I am reduced to the adage, "Write what you know." The world of pornography is so full of wonderful, terrible and terribly wonderful things that I hardly know where to start. There is comfort, certainly, in knowing that I am not alone. My sisters and brothers in Eros have contributed mightily to expanding the understanding of sexually graphic words or pictures. Indeed, one can write a thesis paper or ten using the books on pornography, written with a sympathetic spirit, available right now. What can I possibly add to their inspired, and inspiring, words? What do I bring to the discussion that is new or necessary? It comes down to this: pure experience. Under my g-string I have fourteen years (and counting) of experience stripping, dancing, fucking, sucking, talking, evangelizing, testifying, facilitating, producing, directing and living to tell the tale.

Society Is Still Mystified About Sex

So, what DO I know? I know that my pursuit of sex, both as a livelihood and a spiritual practice, has been well worth any grief that pursuit has caused; that, 30 years of sexual revolution notwithstanding, most people are as confused about and scared of sex as ever. Even after 30 years of improved scientific understanding of sexuality, society is as mystified about it as ever. After three decades of social, legal and religious discourse on sexuality our government and its institutions are as unwilling and unable to modernize their attitudes and actions regarding sexuality as ever. The cauldron of anti-sex hysteria, having simmered for years, is headed toward a full boil, fueled by the issue of child sexuality and the scapegoat du jour, "child pornography." Just as debates over social injustice in the Fifties were instantly derailed by red-baiting, today's debates over issues concerning the rights of adults versus children are silenced by accusations of being "soft on pornography." Unfortunately, the sex-positive community is on the defensive, as yet unable to convince the great middle of America that it is not the boogey man. While those who are sex-negative still set the terms of the debate, still assume that they are right and that God is on their side, it is a fact that an awful lot of Americans jack (or jill) off to porn movies each and every day and night, exorcising their "demons" so that they can face another day of fence-sitting, passing judgment and overlooking social injustice as well as their own deepening alienation. And, while I may be a shining beacon of sanity and goodness to a large number of people, it remains true that many others believe in their soul that I am the devil incarnate.

How do I live with such contradictions? With knowing that I am a lightning rod for the most volatile of emotions? The answer is simple: I do it because I want people to think and talk about sexuality and what it means to them. I believe that sexuality (read: life force) is at the root of our essence as humans and that its perversion by religious fear has created the dire state of our existence today, and that its rehabilitation by the new paganism/tribalism/spirituality could just be our salvation as a species, if not as a culture. I have deliberately made myself available to the public so that people would have someone they could approach easily and talk with about sexuality without fear of derision or rejection, someone who could (and would) give it to them straight. Sexuality had no champion, no one to defend it against the slander aimed at it by the "sex-negatives" and their smug assertion that it was indefensible; no one who could stand up to the vilification without crumbling. I became that person because the means they used, time tested over the centuries, were useless against me. The name calling, the threats of damnation, even casting aspersions on my character, did not have the intended effect, nor could they. "Whore," "Jezebel" and the like can have no negative impact on me since I do not subscribe to traditional sexual mores. Thundering promises of God's displeasure can have no effect on a person sure of her spiritual path. Calling character into question merely because of alternative sexual attitudes cannot faze someone raised on books by Betty Dodson, Xaviera Hollander and The Boston Women's Health Collective.

Pornography Can Save Civilization

What once felt like a lonely battle is lonely no more. There are hundreds of fellow sex-positive feminists, many of them sex workers, as well as writers and scholars who champion this cause. Thanks to our efforts, there is a whole new understanding, mirrored in the popular media, regarding men, women and the graphic display (in words or pictures) of sexual activity. Since openness is now a matter of life and death, not "merely" pleasure, it must be discussed. That anyone still opposes the free and easy dissemination of age-appropriate sexual information only goes to show how far off-track the past five thousand years of history has taken us. The issue has reached a critical mass and the next twenty years will be the most telling. Lines have been drawn, sides chosen, the battle joined. Who will triumph, Eros or Mars, life or death? The finish of the story is ours to determine.

How can that be? The anti-sex folks still run the country and its institutions. Their antiquated, superstitious ideas about non-procreative sex still permeate the laws regarding sexual expression and commerce. Every day people feel the harsh sting of the establishment's lash controlling what goes on in their bedrooms, between their ears or between their legs. How can we prevail against the hegemony of such societal forces? In one word, pornography.

Yes, it is true. Pornography can save civilization. How? Because of pornography's raison d'etre: orgasm. Yep, it can finally be told. After millennia of bad press, the physiological phenomena known as "orgasm" has been shown irrefutably to have no known negative side effects, as long as achieved in a safe, sane and consensual manner. In fact, the beneficial sequelae are still being tallied. How can orgasms save the world? Well, to borrow a phrase used to describe Jazz, "if I have to tell you, you will never know." One either understands "coming" or one does not. Over the years, I have found that the people who have the strongest negative reaction to me are those whose sex lives are less than satisfying. Bluntly put, they are not coming enough and I, who remind them of that fact, am not welcome. It seems to be directly proportionate: the more unhappy a person is with the state of their intimate relations, the more hysterically anti-porn they are. The more sexually satisfied a person is, the more benignly, even positively, they generally regard me. . . . For people who have them, it is easy to see how treating orgasms with more respect for their amazing transformative power, then organizing and focusing that transcendent energy toward a common goal could really shake things up. For people who believe that pleasure is the devil's tool instead of god's, it is easy to see why people like me and my friends signal the end of the world as they know it. All along, they have been told that they need outside assistance in order to connect with God and here we are, saying god is at the end of your arm and as close as your next orgasm.

Sexual Pleasure Is Not Shameful

Still, how can I be so sure about orgasms changing the world? Because orgasms changed me and I can extrapolate from there. I have, as a basis for all my discussions on pornography, the kinesthetic knowledge (supported by extensive scientific data) that orgasms are fundamentally good and anything that promotes them cannot be all bad, no matter how bad parts of it might seem. If the person I am talking to continues to believe that orgasms are anything less than intrinsically good, we can get nowhere. Looking at a photo or video of someone having an orgasm either makes one smile in recognition/remembrance/anticipation or makes one aware of the pleasure/intimacy deficit in one's life and causes one pain. How one chooses to handle such pain is the crux of the matter. If the person enduring pain is in a position of power and influence, that pain can be passed on in the form of laws regulating the expression of sexuality. And, so we come to our society's negative attitude about pornography. Pornography is not ugly; our society's attitudes about sex are ugly. Pornography does not degrade the people in it; our society degrades people for desiring sex. Pornography is not shameful to enjoy; our society says we do not deserve the exquisite pleasure and joy that come from "coming." Pornography is powerful because it dares. Dares to shamelessly expose that which has been kept hidden, dares to give form to nameless desires. Shows life after the sharing of pleasure; shows men and women as equal sexual partners. Makes crass what we have been told is holy; makes sacred what we have been told is disgusting. Shows sexuality that scares us. Grosses us out. Moves us. Pleases us. Angers us. Upsets us. Confuses us, makes us wanna holler, shout, cry, scream, beat the pillows, cover our eyes or come in our hands. It is salt on a wound as well as salve for a tortured soul; a sharp stick poking a caged animal or a soothing lullaby in a rocking chair. Pornography and its offspring, orgasm, can give one strength to resist non-stop lies or can harden one's alienation.

Sexual Egalitarianism

Many sexual materials defy traditional stereotypes of both women and pornography by depicting females as voluntarily, joyfully participating in sexual encounters with men on an equal basis. Procensorship feminists may well view a woman's apparent welcoming of sex with a man as degrading, but this is because of their negative attitudes toward women's ability to make sexual choices. Other viewers are likely to see such a scene as positive and healthy. As feminist lawyer Nan Hunter asked, "What if a woman says to a man, 'fuck me'? Is that begging, or is it demanding? Is she submitting, or is she in control?"

Nadine Strossen, *Defending Pornography: Free Speech, Sex, and the Fight for Women's Rights*, 1995.

Spreading the good news about open sexuality is not only my vocation, it is my avocation. I am an unabashed flag waver for the positive effects of nudism, dance, Jazz, full body massage, swinging and group sex. Being part of the parallel universe of sex-positivism has changed my life for the better and, with no end in sight, I want to spread the word. Whether celibate or "promiscuous," there is some form of sexual expression that is right for you and can (safely) increase your happiness quotient. People often say how much they admire me, how they wish they could be like me, how intimidated they feel by me, or how inspired. I admit, my public persona is potent, seemingly unattainable, but that is not the whole truth. To paraphrase Sophia Loren, "Every thing you see, I owe to pornography." A geek in disguise as well as a recovering situation fuck, I am the way I am because I have worked hard at it. I have been "practicing" sex for eighteen years and studied it for a decade before that. When I was very young, I wanted to become sexually competent and confident and I decided I would let nothing stand in my way, especially my own hang-ups. I wanted to get to the bottom of what was holding me back and kick it out of my life. Therein lies my strength as a spokesperson for sex: in the one area most people are still scared to death of, I have no fear. Instead, I hold out my hand in welcome, ready to pull any interested party over the crevasse into my world. In retrospect, it has been a quest, a spiritual journey, if you will. While I may have started off alone, trying to hack my path through the jungle, I was not alone for long. In 1980 I found my life partners, Dave and Bobby, whose wisdom and support have made the "Nina" my public knows possible. Now, there is a large and growing family of "sex-positives," numbering in the thousands (tens of thousands if you count our fellow travelers). We include swingers, members of the S/M and fetish communities, pagans, pierced folk, tattooed folk, strippers, peepshow folk, pornographers (at least some of us), hippies, beatniks, poets, artists, whores, sluts, masturbators, johns, scholars, exhibitionists, voyeurs and anyone else who believes in sex as a natural, positive part of life. You can join us too and I am here to say, "C'mon in, the water's fine!"

Some Material Is Barely Tolerable

While I champion the cause of pornography, I am fully aware that there is plenty of material produced that is barely tolerable. In fact, I can agree, in part, with the critique and analysis of porn promulgated by anti-porn feminists. A majority of the movies ARE being made by infantile misogynists obsessively reliving their adolescent fixations. This surprises us? We do our best to raise sexually twisted people then act outraged when they create or desire twisted sexual entertainment or release? Puh-leeze. Whom are we fooling? Such brazen illogic would be laughable if it were not so tragic. Too many of our sisters are in bed with the religious right trying to undo us instead of fighting on the sex-positive side and others who should be with us are just plain turned off by most of the product available. I believe that tolerance is key in any democracy; that First Amendment values should be the greater good here. I believe that it is good citizenship to fight, not only for the speech you like, but for the speech you hate. By labeling all material depicting dicks and pussies as "pornography" and, therefore, intrinsically bad, the antis blind themselves to the existence of good pornography, those sexually explicit words and pictures being made by people with a pure heart and good intentions; designed to uplift hopes and aspirations while enriching our experience and advancing understanding, material that can fulfill criteria for art and education as well as pornography. . . .

The Need for Activism

So, where are we? On the one hand, 1997 has been a good year for me. The cover of *U.S. News and World Report* in February; an essay in Jill Nagle's new book, *Whores And Other Feminists*; articles concerning me in *Marie Claire* magazine (April and September), *Men's Journal* (October); a featured role in *Boogie Nights* from New Line Cinema (October) and the *Gauntlet*. I feel I am starting to have some effect on the culture. On the other hand, people still have to live their sexually alternative lives in the closet, for fear of losing their jobs, kids, or marriages. It is still common to assume the worst about a person's morals simply because they may have different ideas or practices in the area of sexuality. It is still common to assume that a sexually-oriented business attracts "bad elements." But, as long as it is confined to consenting adults and is kept private, why should it matter to anyone else?

We need to band together even more tightly; it is truly Us against Them. The "antis" won't stop until they see us dead and buried. We mustn't let them get away with it. Since pornography is generally controlled at the local level, get involved in local politics. City councils decide what publications are carried in the library, how businesses are zoned; school boards decide which text books will be used and which books will be available in the school library. The local level is where one can be heard and has the most impact. The "antis" are counting on you being so complacent and "cummed" out that you won't even bother to show up for meetings. They are counting on the under-30 crowd to not know shit or even give a shit about these issues. Surprise them and prove them wrong.

"Playboy *can be the gateway drug that leads to the crack cocaine of hard-core porn and bizarre sex.*"

Pornography Is Harmful

Rosaline Bush

Pornography harms individuals, families, and society, argues Rosaline Bush in the following viewpoint. Indulgence in semi-nude imagery can progress dangerously to usage of hard-core pornography, sex addiction, and sexual violence, Bush reports. Many pornographers use brutality and humiliation to force women and children to perform illicit acts. Furthermore, children who are exposed to pornography often acquire a warped view of sexuality that stunts their moral and emotional development. Because pornography contributes to immoral and criminal behavior, Bush maintains, it should not be tolerated. Bush is the editor of *Family Voice*, a conservative journal published monthly by Concerned Women for America.

As you read, consider the following questions:

1. According to Bush, what percentage of rapists report that they use pornography regularly?
2. According to Victor Cline, as cited by the author, what is the four-step progression of pornography addiction?
3. In Bush's opinion, what factors have led to society's present problems with pornography and sexual deviance?

Excerpted from "Caught in the Web of Porn: From Victims to Victors," by Rosaline Bush, *Family Voice*, May 1997. Reprinted with permission.

Besides loneliness, I feel sick—like I'm going to throw up—and I tell myself I have to be strong for the children. But that's not all I feel. What I feel mostly is anger. I don't understand why you won't let go of the pornography and the hookers. How could you choose them over the children? How could you choose them over me? You were all I ever wanted. How come I wasn't enough for you?

If you have ever loved anyone caught in the tentacles of pornography, you can relate to Laurie Hall's pain. In a recent interview on *Beverly LaHaye Live*, she discussed her book, *An Affair of the Mind*. In it, Laurie revealed the damage inflicted on her family by her husband's long-term addiction to pornography.

> My husband Jack, a son of missionaries, had once worked at the White House and had been on the staff of a large Baptist church. Starting out with great potential, this "all-American" guy ended up deeply mired in pornography—and leading a double life.

> The signs were a gradual deterioration. He became secretive and angry. As Jack regressed in behavior, he began to withdraw from the children and me. Slowly he lost the ability to think and feel. [I watched] him lose his soul.

The Suffering Family

While the porn addict suffers in isolation, his family reaps the consequences of his sin. Even if the man is able to keep his habit from escalating into a hard-core obsession, the person he becomes is a far cry from the husband and father or son he could have been. He is unable to form a normal loving attachment with his wife. She must always compete with fantasy women who look perfect and do anything and everything he demands. No matter how hard she tries, how much she loves him—no matter how far she will go to please him—it's never enough. Kathy Gallagher tried hard to please her husband, but found that nothing worked.

> About a year after we were married, we moved to Los Angeles where Steve became a deputy sheriff. There was a lot of pressure being a cop. That's when [the trouble] really escalated. One day I stumbled on hard-core—$30 or $40 magazines—and I couldn't believe my eyes. As time went on, layer after layer emerged. X-rated videos . . . porn shops, prostitutes, and massage parlors. It all erupted within that first two

years of marriage. It ruined me.

Steve was so far gone that he was insane with the stuff. . . . They know what they're doing is wrong, but they're obsessed. [At the same time] it eats away the soul of the wife as well as her husband's. His behavior shook everything I was as a person. I thought, "There's something wrong with me. I created this problem. What can I do to fix it?" So I went into damage control—trying to fix my husband—trying to fix myself. I felt like the only one on the planet with this problem. So I kept my mouth shut.

And I did things to impress him. I went all the way [doing things he asked me to do]. I'm ashamed of myself now. Once you come to the Lord and fall away, then it's possible to do things you never dreamed you'd do. I wanted my husband back so badly. I would do anything. . . . It took me years to figure out what an idol he had become to me.

Subtle and Smooth

Kathy and other victims have discovered first-hand that addiction to pornography begins subtly. It alters one's mood in much the same way as drugs. Just as drug addicts require more potent drugs to receive a "high," consumers of pornography must have a more intense experience to achieve the same euphoric feelings as before. *Playboy* can be the gateway drug that leads to the crack cocaine of hard-core porn and bizarre sex.

Some opponents of pornography declare soft-core porn (like *Playboy*) to be more insidious than the hard-core. Because the magazine features well-known writers on various issues, it appears "legitimate" by association. Its centerfolds are portrayed as the "girl next door"—giving men the impression that all women are available for their pleasure—as mere sex objects.

As this philosophy has permeated our society, the *rate of rape* has soared. The American Family Association reports that a woman is raped in the U.S. *every 46 seconds.* Moreover, *86 percent of all rapists admit to using pornography regularly*. Violent pornography evokes two particularly dangerous rape myths: Violence is normal in male-female sexual relations—and women *enjoy* rape. As a result, "not-guilty" verdicts for rapists are frequent, and rape *victims* are often blamed for the crime.

Pornography has been defined as "all sexually oriented material intended primarily to arouse the reader, viewer or listener." Most people associate television's soft-core with HBO or other "adult" cable channels. But pornographic images are just waiting to invade your home—morning, noon, and prime time. Advertisers use sex to sell everything from cosmetics to cars.

And the staples of regular TV seethe with sex—and obscene violence. Midseason prime-time replacements illustrate the depths to which producers will plunge. Promiscuity and sexual profanity abound. . . .

Arguments Against Pornography

Conservative politicians and religious groups, including the Christian Coalition and Family Research Council (FRC), are vocal opponents of pornography, which they say contributes to declining public morality. They say that pornography weakens the institution of marriage and corrupts men by inciting their baser physical drives, drawing them away from such time-honored values as commitment, love and discipline. Pornography irresponsibly presents sex as something that is cheap, sordid and anonymous—and contrary to the values that society should promote at a time when the institution of marriage is already under assault, conservatives say.

Issues and Controversies on File, September 25, 1998.

This type of pornography is legal, unfortunately. However, the soft-core variety of "erotic and semi-nude" is actually more seductive in its methods than hard-core. Obscenity, child porn, broadcast indecency, and pornography deemed harmful to minors *are all still illegal.* Even so, the Enough Is Enough Campaign reported that America "has over 20,000 outlets selling *prosecutable, hard-core pornography*, which would be found illegal by educated citizens in most American communities."

Although soft-core porn nibbles away at the foundation of society like a swarm of termites, hard-core attacks like a voracious beast, gleefully feasting on the heart of its victim. Once a person has tasted hard-core pornography, he is no longer satisfied with nibbling on the soft stuff.

Pornography is a killer. *It kills intimacy; destroys lives; seduces ambition; breaks up families; separates friends; atrophies decency; and worse—it separates the perpetrator from God* (I Cor. 6:9).

A Dangerous Progression

Porn is progressive. Anne can vouch for that. She watched helplessly as pornography destroyed her Christian husband.

> I had dated Greg for three years. But I never knew he had a problem with pornography until we were married. Suddenly it became all too clear. He let me know early on that I didn't measure up sexually. I was never "pretty enough" or "sexy enough." And he became terribly angry if I were too tired for sex. These explosions were rare at first and he would apologize afterward. So of course, I forgave him.
>
> One time—after we had been married only two months—I was lying in bed half-asleep when Greg grabbed me by the ankle and dragged me from the bed. I thought he was going to fling me around the room. Frantically I reached out to catch myself before my head crashed into the floor. Then he stopped and laughed. He was trying to "teach me a lesson" for "daring to go to sleep before giving him sex."
>
> I confronted Greg about his pornography. He promised never to use it again. I so wanted to believe him. But I watched the progression: First magazines, then movies. When movies were not enough, he needed a real person. That led to phone sex. Soon, even that was no longer enough.
>
> In time, I could tell if he had been viewing pornography simply by how he treated me. The smallest thing—from a dinner he didn't like to a disorderly closet shelf—could set him off. I never knew who would come through the door at night—the wonderful man I married or a monster. And I began to feel like a defective piece of machinery.
>
> I wanted to get help, but I didn't want to disgrace my husband. I didn't have any close friends to whom I could turn. Finally, I found a pastor who counseled me through this difficult time. Then my husband faced a choice—his wife or his addiction. He chose the addiction.

Anne's experience aptly proves the theory of Dr. Victor Cline. As a clinical psychologist Dr. Cline has treated approximately 300 sex addicts (96% male). He found that with a few exceptions, pornography *contributed to their deviations* or addictions. Dr. Cline also discovered a four-step progression in pornography involvement:

• Addiction. Once a person gets hooked, he (or she) must keep coming back. Porn's powerful imagery is the basis for fantasizing and self-gratification.

• Escalation. Like drug addiction, pornography requires more. The porn addict requires rougher, more deviant, and more explicit sex to receive a high.

• Desensitization. The addict views acts originally thought shocking, repulsive, or immoral as normal. He thinks "everybody does it."

• Acting out sexually those things he has been exposed to: Exhibitionism, group sex, rape, molestation, incest, voyeurism, visiting prostitutes, homosexual or violent sex.

A Victimless Crime?

Porn producers would be the first to say that pornography is not a crime—and it has no victims. They claim that porn actors—performing everything from sadistic sex to bestiality—are having the time of their lives. But women and children who have been forced to engage in these productions tell a different story. The 1986 *Attorney General's Commission on Pornography* sheds light on this very dark subject.

Judy, a runaway at 13, was befriended by a man who sold her to a pimp. Her pimp seduced women into prostitution by advertising for "models." He offered to be the "agent" of any woman who answered the ads. Next came an offer to pose for soft-core pornography. Then after involving her in an affair, he talked the woman into prostitution "until she could break into legitimate modeling."

If a girl refused, the pimp used "brutal beatings, starvation, captivity, blackmail" and death threats to coerce her. Then he forced her to act in pornographic movies.

Judy escaped from her pimp because of her escalating drug problems. She became useless for prostitution, and he kicked her out. She ended up at age 18—after five years in prostitution and pornography—scarred from beatings, "penniless, homeless, and addicted to heroin."

For eight years, Jackie lived a sexually promiscuous lifestyle as a Playboy Bunny, frequently visiting Hugh Hefner's mansion. During that time she became suicidal. Jackie confessed that the *Playboy* magazines she saw in her home as a child gave her a "distorted image of sexuality."

"It enticed me to throw aside my Judeo-Christian ethic . . . and to practice recreational sex with no commitments," Jackie said. Many "bunnies" used abortion as birth control. And one was forced to have "her reproductive organs removed because of venereal disease." Jackie sees the rise in rape, teen pregnancy, drug abuse, abortion, and sexually transmitted diseases as a result of the *Playboy* philosophy.

"It took me close to 20 years," she said, "to undo what was done to me in pornography."

The Truth About Porn "Stars"

I.S. Levine—who has directed more than 150 porn movies— said, "The public's idea about this industry is probably not far removed from the kind of industry it is." He described it as, "Exploitive, with marginal personalities, who can't integrate into society—self-destructive people living self-destructive lives." Mr. Levine has a good point. But Concerned Women for America believes that many of the people involved—especially women and children—*did not choose* to participate.

During the early 70s, after the filming of the movie *Deep Throat*, "Linda Lovelace" became a porn "star" overnight. Since that time, Linda Lovelace Marchiano has written her autobiography. In *Ordeal* she reveals that her (then-) husband Charles Trainor forced her to act in the movie. "There were guns, knives, beatings, threats on the lives of my family constantly. And after the physical abuse, the mental abuse becomes just as damaging," Marchiano said. "I think it's important that people realize that. People who produce these films will say, 'Well, we check it out and make sure that these women are doing it willingly.'" But Marchiano noted: "Virtually every time someone watches that film, *they are watching me being raped.*"

These horrendous things don't just happen to "professionals." Some women who appeared before the Attorney General's Commission on Pornography confessed that they had become porn "stars" without their consent or knowledge. Several said their husbands took sexually explicit photos or videos of them—then sold them to porn distributors.

Others told how their husbands captured their sexual abuse or torture on video. These recorded illicit and illegal activities are still being passed around by pornographers. It should be evident to everyone that coercion—used to humiliate, silence, and blackmail women and children—is the backbone of the pornography industry.

Children and Pornography

There is no more dangerous mix than children and pornography. The results are always explosive—and can easily lead to life-long addiction. Children may become involved in pornography at home either through ignorant or permissive parents.

Some people believe that children are too young to understand pornography. Therefore, they have no qualms about leaving magazines lying around, taking a three-year-old to an R-movie, or viewing "sexy" videos at home. But powerful images are burned into children's brains. And since young children can't discern fact from fantasy, what they see is "normal."

Children often discover pornography on their own if a parent or older sibling is a user. The average age of discovery is 11. Children introduced to pornography at this early age are forced into an adult world that they're not ready for. And since their latency period is skipped, many of these adults never mature emotionally.

Children may spend years feeling guilt and shame. Only intervention can prevent them from growing up with a warped view of sex—and the inability to make mature judgments.

About *70 percent of all pornographic magazines and videos end up in the hands of children.* That is especially frightening in light of Richard Restak's research. In his book, *The Brain*, Restak reported that in 3/10 of a second a visual image passes from the eye through the brain, and whether or not one wants to, the brain is structurally changed and memories are created—we literally "grow a new brain" with each visual experience.

Researcher and author Dr. Judith Reisman agrees, "We have no choice—we are designed to believe what we see . . . *fantasy is reality to the human brain.*"

Showing pornography to a child is a favorite ploy of pedophiles. They use it to break down the child's natural inhibitions. Pedophiles often pose as friends, gaining the confidence of children.

Once they have these youngsters in their grasp, they can force them to do anything—often filming the process for posterity. Many of them use pornography to prime themselves for the victimization and then use it in the actual molestation. Afterwards, pedophiles use the photos or videos to prevent the child from telling.

Child porn does not exist without innocent victims—they suffer scarred bodies, as well as permanently damaged minds and emotions.

For every pornographic photo or video is a record of child molestation.

Yet today these perverts are being accepted into America's mainstream, particularly through the media. Recent articles in *Vanity Fair* and *The New Republic* magazines seem to encourage sympathy for pedophiles—rather than exposing them as predators of our children.

And a recent book is being praised because of its "chic" subject—father-daughter incest.

The most well-known group of pedophiles—the National Man-Boy Love Association (NAMBLA)—believes that every child has a "right" to sex.

How have we allowed these vermin to victimize our children? Why have we listened when they say that children not only "like sex," but it is their "right"?

One notorious predator recently had a movie made of his life. *Hustler* publisher Larry Flynt has built an empire around perverted sex.

Touted as a hero of the First Amendment, Flynt was *not* a hero at home. In an interview on *Beverly LaHaye Live*, his daughter, Tonya Flynt-Vega, revealed that her father had beaten, emotionally traumatized, and sexually molested her as a child.

Frightening Facts

• One young girl was physically and sexually tortured by her stepfather because she was not "convincing" in a porn movie.

• A five-year-old told her foster mother, "Daddy and I take our clothes off and do what they do in the movies."

• A Miami pre-schooler who was molested by day care personnel and used in the production of pornography had to undergo psychotherapy.

• One young man who had been forced to act in a pornographic film said he was publicly humiliated when his name came out during a trial. He was only 11 at the time.

If you still think pornography is a victimless crime, read on. . . . According to the Enough Is Enough Campaign:

• 87% of convicted molesters of girls and 77% of convicted molesters of boys admit to the use of pornography, most often in the commission of their crimes.

• An average serial child molester victimizes between 360–380 youngsters in his lifetime.

• 29% of all forcible rapes are against children under the age of 11.

• One in three American girls and one in seven boys will be sexually molested by age 18.

• 22% of boys and 23% of girls who are sexually abused are abused before age eight. . . .

The Roots of the Problem

The rugged individualism so admired in America has gone awry. Husbands shuck family responsibilities to seek fulfillment. Abandoned wives turn to other men to validate their self-worth. Live-in boyfriends introduce children to pornography—or worse, to sex. Without love, nurture, and discipline, children grow up like tough weeds. The result is a deep crack in our cultural foundation.

Our educational system has compounded the foundational fissure. By undermining parental authority, schools have further separated children from families. And sex education classes—beginning in kindergarten—bombard them with information they are not ready for. These emphasize vice over virtue—and condoms over character. AIDS education classes leave nothing to children's imagination—often indoctrinating them into a deviant lifestyle. Why *not* pornography? Why *not* perversion? It's their choice!

Unfortunately, few churches address this problem. Seldom are the subjects of sexual purity or pornography mentioned from the pulpit. Some mainline churches even ordain homosexuals as pastors—while turning a blind eye to adulterers. What does that say to our children? Since we have stopped believing in the degradation of sin or the reality of heaven and hell, there is nothing to stop us from the "pleasures" and perversity of porn and sexual immorality.

We can put band-aids on these sores of sexual sins, but the wounds of the victim and the victimizer can only be healed one way—*from the inside out by Jesus Christ.*

> *"There is no difference in work in which a woman sells her hands, such as a typist, and work in which a woman sells her vagina, as in sex work."*

Prostitution Should Be Decriminalized

Lacey Sloan

Lacey Sloan is a professor in the Graduate School of Social Work at the University of Houston. In the following viewpoint, Sloan presents an argument supporting the decriminalization of prostitution. In her view, women in the sex-trade industry are entrepreneurs who should be granted the same rights as workers in other fields. Fully legalizing prostitution would help protect sex workers from the abuse and exploitation that permeates the illegal sex-trade industry. Moreover, contends Sloan, sex work can be empowering because it enables women to assert their sexuality for their own purposes.

As you read, consider the following questions:

1. According to Sloan, what two groups have set the terms of the current debate over the status of prostitutes?
2. What happened in 1973 that raised awareness about the abuse of sex workers by civil authorities?
3. For what reasons does the author prefer decriminalizing prostitution instead of regulating it?

Excerpted from "Who Owns Prostitution—and Why?" by Lacey Sloan, *Free Inquiry*, Fall 1997. Reprinted with permission.

Prostitution is a crime—or is it a business? Its practitioners are victims—or are they entrepreneurs? They're oppressed—or are they rulers of their own destiny?

So it goes—and has gone for centuries—in the debate over the status of prostitutes and their maligned profession.

The Debate

Nowadays, the verbal conflict exists primarily between some feminists and women escaping the sex-trade industry (all forms of sex work) on one side, and other feminists and women in the sex-trade industry who want to be considered legitimate workers on the other side. Although many people believe that all feminists recognize sex work (sexual activity performed for compensation) as victimization, women who consider themselves feminists do not all speak with the same voice on this issue.

Almost all feminists and sex workers who have written on the subject advocate that sex workers not be criminally liable for engaging in sex work. Almost all feminists and sex workers also acknowledge the abuse endured by sex workers and the poor social, political, and economic condition of women in general. Beyond these similarities, two distinct points of view emerge. On one side are feminists and women escaping the sex-trade industry who believe that sex work is a form of victimization of women perpetrated by a patriarchal system that wants to maintain men's right to sexual access to women. This group of women (frequently referred to as prostitution abolitionists) believes sex workers are victims and call for the abolition of the sex-trade industry (sex work would be legal, but procuring, pimping, and profiting from the wages of a sex worker would not). On the other side of the debate, other feminists and sex-trade workers (frequently referred to as sex-workers' rights groups) claim sex workers are businesswomen who should be granted the same freedom to work as any other worker. These sex-workers' rights groups claim sex workers are not victims, except of puritanical mores and oppressive laws; they want sex work legalized or decriminalized.

Prior to 1973, sex workers were not acknowledged as being capable of speaking for themselves. In 1973, Margo St. James organized a sex-workers' rights organization called

COYOTE (Call Off Your Old Tired Ethics). Together with a variety of professionals, including social workers, sex workers have tried to raise awareness about the abuse of sex workers by the state and police, and to effect changes in laws.

By the mid-1970s, sex-workers' rights organizations began to form across the United States and around the world (for example, in The Netherlands, the Red Thread; in Atlanta, Georgia, Hooking Is Real Employment [HIRE]; and, in England, Prostitution Laws Are Nonsense [PLAN]). Sex-workers' rights groups believe that "most women who work as prostitutes have made a conscious decision to do so, having looked at a number of work alternatives." These organizations, along with the American Civil Liberties Union (ACLU) and the National Organization for Women (NOW), want sex work decriminalized or legalized. These groups believe that the illegal status of most sex-trade workers leaves these women unprotected from acts of violence, rape, and exploitation.

The advent of the sex-workers' rights movement of the 1970s finally provided a forum for the sex worker to speak for herself. The sex-workers' rights movement was founded on three general tenets, all of which are based on the right to self-determination. First, members of the movement do not believe that all sex work is forced, and, in fact, believe that many women freely choose this work. Second, they believe that sex work should be viewed and respected as legitimate work. And third, they believe it is a violation of a woman's civil rights to be denied the opportunity to work as a sex worker. These women "demand recognition as workers" as well as "freedom to financial autonomy . . . occupational choice . . . sexual self-determination . . . (and) worker's rights and protections."

Contrary to the abolitionists' plan to support sex workers while working to eliminate the institution of sex work, sex-workers' rights groups and many sex workers reject "support which requires them to leave the profession." They also "object to being treated as symbols of oppression," an image placed on them by some authors. Sex-workers' rights groups claim there is no difference in work in which a woman sells her hands, such as a typist, and work in which a woman sells her vagina, as in sex work.

Concerns About Violence and Exploitation

Sex workers and sex-workers' rights groups are concerned about the sexual violence, physical violence, and/or exploitation that prostitutes suffer at the hands of customers, pimps, and the police. As sex workers spoke out at the World Whores Congresses, many told of heinous acts of abuse that had been perpetrated against them and other prostitutes. They acknowledged that sex workers have been kidnapped, tortured, raped, and forced into sex work. Yet, unlike those who rally for the abolition of sex work, those in favor of decriminalization (which would make all aspects of sex work legal, but perhaps subject to standard business regulations) want these abuses stopped by the enforcement of existing laws that prohibit kidnapping, assault, rape, and fraud. Those who support the decriminalization of prostitution and other forms of sex work point to the illegality of most sex work as one of the primary factors that leaves them vulnerable to abuse, rape, and exploitation.

Women Must Have Sovereignty over Their Bodies

The deepening schism between prostitute activists and anti-prostitution feminists further separates the two camps, who should be natural allies rather than enemies. Feminism, which once championed the cause of choice and freedom, has become an unwitting oppressor of women. Feminism, at its core, seeks equality for women in every arena of society. Yet a feminism that calls for choice when it comes to abortion, but interference when it comes to prostitution, will eventually topple under the weight of that contradiction. Women must be free to choose their own lives and must have sovereignty over their own bodies, even when those choices and that sovereignty challenge mainstream mores.

Wendy McElroy, *Liberty*, January 1999.

In countries where sex work is regulated, sex workers are stigmatized and placed under scrutiny not required of any other legal worker. Other forms of control enforced in regulated systems include registration of sex workers and "imprisonment" in brothels or within certain zones. In countries and states where sex work is illegal and/or tolerated (authorities ignore or loosely enforce the laws), sex workers are unable to demand rights and benefits as workers and are generally denied police protection. This leaves sex workers vulnerable to exploitation, poor working conditions, physical abuse, arrest, and incarceration. Immigrant women who prostitute may be deported; mothers who prostitute can lose custody of their children. These are but a few examples of the reasons sex workers want prostitution (sexual activity involving direct contact with customers for compensation) and sex work decriminalized, not regulated or prohibited (complete criminalization).

Empowerment for All Women

Sex workers and sex workers' rights groups reject the notion that female heterosexuality perpetuates male privilege and men's dominance of women. Many sex workers believe that it empowers all women for sex workers to charge men for what men expect all women to provide for free. This conflicts with the view that the sex-trade industry perpetuates men's belief in their right to sexual access to all women. The editors of the 1983 text *Powers of Desire: The Politics of Sexuality* stated that,

> [Blinded] by their own experiences as middle-class women, the social purity feminists were entirely unable to perceive the ways in which other women—their own working class sisters—could act as sexual agents rather than as victims, using sex to further their own purposes and pleasures.

Sex workers, prostitutes' rights groups, social workers, and others working for decriminalization point to the history of control of prostitution to reveal that most methods adopted to protect and support prostitutes, such as regulation (legalizing but licensing, taxing, and imposing rules for operation), have failed. Initiatives to prohibit sex work or prostitution have resulted in the isolation, increased vulnerability, abuse, and exploitation of sex work. Programs to regulate sex work have resulted in the control and further stigmatization of sex workers. And, finally, efforts to abolish sex work have denied sex workers their rights to autonomy and self-determination.

"Sex work . . . perpetuates the notion that women's bodies exist for male sexual gratification, not for our own."

Prostitution Demeans Women

Nell Beram

Prostitution and other forms of sex work are not empowering for women, argues Nell Beram in the following viewpoint. Many feminist supporters of prostitution have argued that sex work grants women control over their own sexuality. In actuality, Beram contends, a female sex worker is controlled by the desires of the man who purchases her services. Prostitution is demeaning because it reinforces the antifeminist idea that women are basically objects of male sexual desire, maintains the author. Beram, a graduate of the Iowa Writers Workshop, is assistant editor of the *Hungry Mind Review*.

As you read, consider the following questions:
1. According to Beram, what would happen if a prostitute really was in control of her own sexuality when she sold her body?
2. What is wrong with the feminist economic defense of sex work, in the author's view?
3. In Beram's opinion, why do nearly all male and female prostitutes serve men?

Reprinted, with permission, from "Sex Work and Feminism," by Nell Beram, *Z Magazine*, March 1998.

I had no money. In the middle of the night, the landlord would call me up to demand the back months' rent. After a while, I did not answer the phone so late at night. I looked for a job, but I was not qualified to do anything respectable. . . . In this apartment, I slept with a man who used to buy me dinner. I liked fish of every kind. When I went out with him, it was only to eat fish. . . . Most of what we did together was inside the apartment, and that was soon over.

—Jamaica Kincaid, from "Putting Myself Together," an autobiographical essay

In the bookstore where I work part time, the women's studies section is spattered with titles like: *Live Sex Acts: Women Performing Erotic Labor*; *Sex Work: Writings by Women in the Sex Industry*; and *Whores and Other Feminists*. As I understand it, the author and editors of—and some contributors to—these books identify as feminists, and I'm thankful for the company: the greater the number of tentacles, the harder our tent is to topple. I'd value novelist Jamaica Kincaid's nod as well.

I believe absolutely that women (and men) and not their kin or governments have the right to sovereignty over their own bodies. Yet the long-term yield of the social sanctioning of cosmetic surgery, for example, troubles me: a long, classically Semitic nose (like mine) will become that much more of an aberration every time somebody has hers or his shortened. (If there were an equal number of nose augmentations going on I wouldn't be making this fuss.) The curve on the "attractive nose" graph changes shape and we become a culture in which the brackets defining the day's standards of beauty contract.

Who Controls a Sex Worker's Body?

Although I don't know any sex workers personally—at least no one has ever confided as much to me—I do buy the prevailing notion that many women who become sex workers consider themselves desperate. But as Heidi Mattson, author of *Ivy League Stripper*, and novelist and former prostitute Mary Gaitskill attest, indeed there are some basically middle-class, drug-free women whose service as sex workers doesn't result from destitution. According to the books I've listed, some women (not just Camille Paglia) believe that sex work is a feminist enterprise because (a) by casting themselves as sexual objects, women are for once "in control" of their sexuality, and because (b) they are not beholden to husbands, boyfriends, or governments for their meal tickets.

The "tables turned" justification of sex work confounds me. Because she depends on his arousal, a prostitute is implicitly controlled by her john, a stripper by her (male) audience, no matter the surface nature of the exchange bought with his dollar (e.g., she dominatrix, he helpless conquest). If she were in control, her sexual pleasure would be part of the barter; as Lillian S. Robinson notes in her review of *Live Sex Acts* in the October 1997 issue of *The Women's Review of Books*, "[author Wendy] Chapkis . . . persists in treating prostitution as these women's sexual identity, even though they testify to faking it."

As for the economic defense of sex work, it presumes that feminism is about economic equity at the expense of all else. Thirty years after the second wave and on the heels of some incontrovertible feminist victories (*Roe v. Wade*, public acknowledgment of sexual harassment as a real phenomenon), why are our sights so low? Poet Audre Lorde might have been thinking of pro-sex-work feminists when she wrote her famous speech, "The Master's Tools Will Never Dismantle the Master's House," whose pertinent next line is, "They may allow us temporarily to beat him at his own game, but they will never enable us to bring about genuine change."

Reinforcing Male Entitlement

I think it's crucial to realize the shortsightedness of the sex-work alternative: the idea that women are gladly in sexual servitude to men in exchange for money reinforces a climate of male entitlement under which all women, present and future, must live. Do men understand that the women who are telling them they like it are actors hiding their natural impulses beneath the garments and personae of his choosing? What can these men be teaching their sons about female sexuality?

Perhaps if there were equal numbers of male and female sex workers I wouldn't be so testy. (Prostitute, like nurse, is a job title that must be modified by the adjective "male" before this possibility will occur to the average brain.) It isn't due to the mythical male sex drive that nearly all prostitutes of both sexes serve men; it's because men have most of the money.

When more women have money to burn, prostitutes, male and female, and proprietors of strip clubs will no doubt more actively court us. Perhaps not the most compelling reason to take out our scythes and level that playing field, but a sign that we are encroaching on parity just the same.

© Joseph Shoopack.

Still, can money be a fair trade for access to another's body, an entity that I don't believe can alternate between having value some days (hours, minutes) and no value others, depending on the solicitor. In the words of WHISPER (Women

Hurt In Systems of Prostitution Engaged in Revolt) founder Evelina Giobbe, "How can we say, it's your body, your self—and suddenly it's for sale?" We can't shed our skins like *Miami Vice* pastels when they begin to repel us.

Sex Work Is Anti-Feminist

You've heard of the woman who turns to stripping or prostitution to finance her law school education—after all, sex work is lucrative. Who knows? She may even dedicate her practice to helping women prosecute men who mistreat them—women whose psychic duress has likely interfered with their own careers. But what of our lawyer's means to this professional end? Are we certain that a man who paid for her sexual services didn't interpret her subservience as a feature of women generally? Do we know where all the men who mistreat the women seeking our lawyer's counsel come from?

I won't deceive you: I often wish I had a modest little nose. But I'm staying out of scalpel's reach because I believe cosmetic surgery necessarily threatens diversity in that it narrows the parameters around what physically "normal" is in our culture. I'm grateful for my choices, however, and it would be philosophically inconsistent of me to argue against the legalization of prostitution. But even ignoring the drug addiction and health risks that often accompany it, I see sex work as necessarily anti-feminist in that it perpetuates the notion that women's bodies exist for male sexual gratification, not for our own. How do we explain the existence of pro-sex-work feminists to those laudable men who are working to challenge their own eons-old feelings of entitlement?

I keep thinking about Jamaica Kincaid, who did not find sleeping with a man she did not care for in exchange for food less "respectable" than her other employment options. If we can't have a moratorium on so-called sex work, can we at least have a moratorium on this declawed euphemism? And can we remind ourselves that feminism has never been about the sovereignty of one woman over her landlord but about the safety and self-respect of us all?

"Evolutionarily, we're built to have multiple relationships. . . . We're built to fool around."

Multiple Relationships Are a Legitimate Alternative to Monogamous Marriage

Alicia Potter

Polyamory—the practice of having more than one love relationship with the knowledge and consent of all partners—is a feasible alternative to monogamy, maintains Alicia Potter in the following viewpoint. Emphasizing the importance of relationships and honesty rather than sexual variety, polyamorists are able to share the different aspects of themselves with their different partners. This, Potter points out, diffuses the pressure that monogamous individuals often feel to meet all of their partner's needs. Like monogamous marriages, polyamorous relationships can become lifelong commitments in which partners share living space, economic resources, and child-rearing responsibilities. Potter is a freelance writer living in Boston.

As you read, consider the following questions:
1. According to Potter, what is the difference between polyamory and swinging?
2. What percentage of all animal species are sexually monogamous, according to the author?
3. How does Megan O'Neal, quoted by Potter, deal with jealousy in her polyamorous relationships?

Excerpted from "Free Love Grows Up," by Alicia Potter, *The Boston Phoenix*, October 5–12, 1998. Reprinted by permission of the author.

On a crooked street in Somerville, Massachusetts, is a purple house that no doubt raises eyebrows every few Thursdays. That's when it becomes a meeting site for Love Without Bounds, a local organization for young believers in free love.

On a recent evening, members of the group arrive in boisterous trios and hand-holding twosomes. They greet each other with deep, lingering embraces—no air kisses here—before plunking onto pillows or curling up together in corners. If ever a crowd spelled "orgy," it's this one.

But two hours pass, and the gathering fails to erupt into any sort of carnal acrobatics. At least the conversation is provocative, but again, not in the way you might think.

"Sex is cheap," says a black-clad man, to nods of agreement. "I want *relationships*."

It feels like a big book club, with slightly different topics of conversation. The members talk about how to ask someone out if you're married. How to fend off jealousy if you're living with your lover and *his* lover. How to deal with a world of pairs when you're part of a trio. In short, they talk about what it's like to be polyamorous.

What Is Polyamory?

Polyamory is the philosophy and practice of loving more than one person at a time. It's different from polygamy—the practice of taking more than one wife—in that polyamory is legal, has nothing to do with Mormonism, and spans a whole range of commitment levels besides marriage. The possibilities are endless; as one 32-year-old man, married, with a child and a lover, puts it, "You don't have to end a relationship to start a new one." Some polyamorists share a household with two or more common-law spouses; others have one "primary" partner, often a legal spouse, and one or more secondary relationships beyond that. There are triads [a polyamorous relationship in which all three lovers are involved with one another] and Vs [a polyamorous relationship in which one person has two lovers but the lovers are not involved with each other]. The only requirement is that all involved agree on the ground rules.

Polyamorists will point out that the practice has been

around for much, if not all, of human history; in the Book of Genesis, for instance, Sarah lets Abraham beget children with her maid Hagar. Our own culture is steadfastly monogamous, but statistics hint that humans and monogamy can be an uneasy marriage: 25 to 60 percent of American men commit adultery, as do 15 to 40 percent of women. Half of all marriages end in divorce. Fourteen percent of all weddings include someone who's tying the knot for the third time.

For the people in this purple house, monogamy isn't a goal; it's a point of departure. And sex, while an important part of the equation, isn't the point. The point is to find an alternative to monogamy that's less restrictive, but just as stable. The Love Without Bounds members talk about commitment and communication and responsibility with the sort of earnestness that we associate with a couples-therapy session. And, as impossible as it may sound, they are hoping for mainstream recognition.

Support for Polyamory

Boston may be just the place to find it. The area is already home to an active bisexual community, which intersects with the polyamory scene; it's also the birthplace of Family Tree, one of the nation's oldest polyamory support groups, founded in 1975 and still flourishing.

For now, though, the quest for recognition isn't primarily political. It's personal. "Coming out" is a hot topic among the 25 Love Without Bounds members crowded into this tiny living room.

"I can say I'm bisexual and everyone knows what that is," says Lisa, 26, who asked that only her first name be used. "People may not like it . . . but I don't have to spend 20 minutes defining it. One day, I'd just like to say, 'Hi, I'm poly.'"

Poly lesson number one: the proper response to such an introduction is not "That's the same thing as swinging, right?"

"Swinging is impersonal sex," says Deborah M. Anapol of San Rafael, California, author of *Polyamory: The New Love Without Limits*. "And while I'm not judging that, I don't consider it polyamory, because it doesn't focus on the relationship."

In fact, ask people why they became involved with polyamory and you won't hear much about spouse-swapping or other libidinal adventures (though, yes, threesomes and foursomes do occur). More likely, you'll hear love stories. Complex love stories.

"There are two people who I think are really special, who I want to spend a lot of time with," says a 32-year-old man who's involved with two women. "It's wonderful to have a way to do that."

Sean Sullivan, 26, agrees. A slight man who looks a little like Jesus, he's been involved for four and a half years with Tamara, a bespectacled redhead whom he met as a freshman at Amherst College. That same year, three of his friends entered into a polyamorous relationship, a triad made up of two women and one man. Their closeness intrigued him: currently, he's involved with one of the women, while Tamara has recently started dating a second man. Soon, Sullivan hopes to house all the relationships under one roof.

Marriage Plus More

There doesn't seem to be a "typical" poly relationship. Triads and Vs are popular among the polys I spoke to, with a long-distance lover here or there. Foursomes—say, a relationship with two married couples—are reportedly the hardest to pull off: first, both spouses must find a couple they like *that* much, and second, the intensity is difficult to balance (the husband may be smitten with the other woman more than his wife is smitten with the other man, for example). In the poly world, four really can be a crowd. But when the relationships work, whether with three or four or (in Sullivan's case) six, there's a payoff.

"Poly can be a marriage plus more," says Sullivan. "It can be a lifelong partnership [in which] people live together, help raise children together, grow old together. All of the things people speak of when they speak of family values apply even more to polyamory."

Idealistic? Sure. But perhaps no more so than the talk of heart-eyed romantics bent on finding "the One." Data show, too, that Sullivan's vision isn't all that deluded: Arline M. Rubin, of Brooklyn College, has conducted a 20-year study of polyamorous couples and has found that their relationships last just as long as supposedly monogamous ones. Among Family Tree's 75 members are polyamorous grandparents who enjoy not only 40-year-old marriages but also secondary relationships spanning 15 years.

Such commitment is possible, polys say, because their lifestyle diffuses a lot of relationship pressures. Banish the concept of "my one and only," and you lift the burden of meeting all of a lover's emotional and intellectual needs. In essence, polys are free to choose their paramours as most of us choose our friends: as complements to different sides of their personalities. One lover may share a spiritual outlook, another an ironic sense of humor, another a passion for horror movies.

Says Sullivan: "It allows for stronger emotional bonds than I'd have otherwise. I think if I was in a single relationship there would probably be aspects of myself that I wouldn't really be able to share with just one person. Additional relationships mean there's more of myself I can express."

He scratches his thick beard and shrugs. "There's just more companionship.". . .

We Are All Potentially Polyamorous

"For me it's not a question of loving polyamory," says Alan Wexelblat, 36, who in 18 years of dating has always had poly relationships. "It's who I am. Even if I were only in one relationship and following monogamous rules, that doesn't change me, just like a bisexual person can be in a relationship with any one person and yet still be identified as bisexual."

It's an interesting idea, especially given the inability of many people to stay reliably within the constraints of monogamy: could it be that those cheating louts are polyamorous but just don't know it?

Likely so, says anthropologist Helen Fisher, author of *Anatomy of Love: A Natural History of Mating, Marriage, and Why We Stray*. But they're not the only ones: we're all potentially polyamorous.

"You would think that more people would be [practicing] polyamory, because, evolutionarily, we're built to have multiple relationships," she says. "We're built to fool around."

Anthropologists now believe that, at the most, 2 percent of all species are completely faithful sexually (among them the Nile crocodile, the American toad, the dung beetle, and some desert wood lice). In her book, Fisher points out that anthropological studies of 853 human societies showed only 16 percent practicing monogamy as we typically define it. And, as we know, even monogamy doesn't guarantee fidelity; in many of the monogamous cultures, researchers discovered covert or tolerated affairs.

Group Marriage

One of the most popular styles of polyamory is polyfidelity, sometimes also called closed group marriage. In polyfidelity, groups of three or more lovers consider themselves essentially married to each other. They usually live together in a single home and share their life and resources such as married couples do. There may be any combination of males, females and sexual orientations. Polygamy, as it was practiced by the original Mormon, was just one example of polyfidelity. Classically, polyfide groups are sexually exclusive and do not engage in sexual relations outside the group. However, there are some group marriages which are "open," and which do allow for outside eromances.

Larry Smith, www.twomoons.com/poly/polyintr.htm, June 24, 1999.

Fisher has an explanation for our longings: she says that our brain circuitry has evolved so that the chemical reactions associated with different kinds of love—attachment, infatuation, lust—function independently of one another. In other words, we can find comfort with an old lover, flirt with a cute coworker, and fantasize about that beautiful stranger—all in the course of an hour.

"However," Fisher cautions, "we're not built to share. We get jealous. That puts the human animal in a pickle."

Polyamorists, she says, have found a way out. "They're honestly dealing with the fact that we're not built to be faithful," she explains. "They accept that inevitability and channel it in ways that minimize pain and maximize joy. They attempt paradise."

This paradise, though, can be very unfamiliar territory. Take this scene, for example: Rob Mohns, 25, nuzzles his girlfriend Aileen, 22, while two feet away, knitting a scarf, is his fiancée, 26-year-old Megan O'Neal. As Mohns and his new love practically roll off the couch, O'Neal's face is serene.

"I don't usually get jealous," says O'Neal. "And when I do, it takes me by surprise. It's kind of good, because it usually means that something in this situation isn't working for me, that I need to figure out what it is and go talk to the person."

Spend some time with polyamorists and you realize that communication is what keeps their relationships alive. Polys talk about *everything:* who they want to go out with, what they do on their dates, how their relationships are progressing.

Poly commitments give new meaning to "the Rules." To the average monogamist, some of these relationship statutes might seem mind-boggling: as a polyamorist, for example, you might negotiate whether or not your lover can sleep with another in your bed. Other rules are kind of silly: one man's girlfriend asked that he accompany only her to first-run movies. Safe sex—condoms, dental dams—is a given; a long-time Family Tree member reports that in nearly 25 years, there has been only one sexually-transmitted-disease scare, and that was a false alarm. But many guidelines are simple and practical: no surprises, no keeping secrets with secondary lovers, and no cheating, which in this context means you don't get involved with someone new without apprising the others.

"No, we're not running around doing whatever we damn well please," says Aileen. "We have to talk about things and be open. If we don't, it's disastrous." In that respect, monogamy and polyamory have a lot in common.

"Cultures that fail to support monogamous marriage lose the generative vibrancy that comes from commitment and deferred gratification which, along with love, make marriages possible."

Multiple Relationships Are Not a Legitimate Alternative to Monogamous Marriage

Robert H. Knight

Polyamory—the practice of consensual nonmonogamy—does not deserve the support of mainstream American society, proclaims Robert H. Knight in the following viewpoint. Sexuality that occurs outside the conventional marital relationship leads to emotional scars and myriad social ills, including sexually transmitted diseases and broken families, Knight contends. The deep level of commitment and self-sacrifice that monogamous marriage entails provides the optimum environment for a healthy family life, which is the basis of a stable culture, he concludes. Knight is the director of cultural studies at the Family Research Council, a conservative advocacy organization.

As you read, consider the following questions:

1. In Knight's opinion, what is the rationale behind polyamorous relationships?
2. Why are definable bloodlines and inheritance rights important for civilizations, in the author's view?
3. According to Knight, what biblical evidence provides strong support for monogamous marriages?

Polyamourous Family Redefines Tradition," proclaimed the front-page story in the *Daily Iowan* early in 1998. But the headline is a little misleading. The four bisexuals—Tina, Dawn, Troy and Lon—are not interested in tradition, except to make clear that tradition is an impediment to their happiness. It is precisely their casting aside of the traditional notions of marriage, family and monogamy that has landed them on the front page of a progressive daily newspaper.

To some, smashing traditions is the same as creating new ones. And if the trendier cultural scribes are good at anything, it is creating oxymorons such as new traditions, otherwise known as fads. In a less-congratulatory tone, the *New York Times Magazine* carried an article on "polyluv," which is a lifestyle name for group sex. In Boulder, Colorado, and in San Francisco, adherents of polyluv are given exercises in "jealousy comparison challenge" (visualizing being happy that your mate is sleeping with somebody else). Some groups now are getting married, the *Times* reports, and ordering wedding cakes—with six figurines.

Flouting Normalcy

As part of Queer Harvard Month, the Fifth International Bisexual Conference in April 1998 featured presentations such as "Polyamourous Paths: Loving More Than One." Workshop presenter Jay Sekora, self-described as poly since he was old enough to think about relationships, was joined by Elena Wyldheart, a specialist in tantric and sexual-healing workshops whose passion is leading groups into the sacred realms of deep body/soul communion. Together with several other presenters, they explored how consensual nonmonogamous relationships fit into our lives.

During the debate in Congress about the Defense of Marriage Act, Oklahoma Republican Sen. Don Nickles and others warned that destroying the definition of marriage from a one-man, one-woman relationship would lead not only to homosexual marriage but to the acceptance of polygamy. Polyluv folks are proving the senator's point.

The Iowa foursome even are raising an 11-month-old boy, whom the *Daily Iowan* identifies only as Rowan. The boy's last name is a mystery. No matter. The business at hand is to validate the flouting of normalcy. As *Daily Iowan* reporter Jeff Clayton writes: "Despite their nontraditional lifestyle, they successfully function as a family unit. They cook, clean and raise a child just the same as a nuclear family."

Errant Sex Leads to Disaster

Just the same? If that were the case, there would be no story. But why quibble? The point is that the arrangement makes the adults happy. As Dawn notes, "If I'm not up to this (attending to Rowan), there are three other people." The situation, she notes, alleviates stress by giving everyone time to themselves, allowing them to live healthier and happier lives. Of course, that is the same rationale that some day-care proponents use to justify leaving young children in the care of strangers from sunrise to bedtime: so the parents can be more fulfilled. This is supposed to make them better parents (it takes a village, you know—or maybe just a couple more parents).

Truth be told, there are few mothers anywhere, or even some fathers, who do not long for some help during the arsenic hour when dinner isn't ready, the phone is ringing and the kids are fighting and crying. But the answer is not to create a collective bedroom for group sex. For thousands of years, children raised in two-parent, mom-and-dad homes have fared significantly better than children in all other alternative arrangements.

This is no accident or mere conventionality. When sexuality occurs outside the marital relationship there is hell to pay, as evidenced by the wreckage from no-fault divorce, premarital sex, adultery and homosexual sex. The litany of social ills from errant sex is well documented, from venereal diseases to shattered families. The full extent of the emotional damage can never be calculated.

The Importance of Monogamous Marriage

There is magic in the way a husband and wife, a father and mother—one man and one woman—relate that creates an optimum family environment for children. The idea that sexuality is a minor point is belied by thousands of years of human history. Cultures that fail to support monogamous marriage lose the generative vibrancy that comes from commitment and deferred gratification which, along with love, make marriages possible. Without marriage and kinship, without definable bloodlines and inheritance rights, there is less reason to build for the future.

CREAK!

In both the Old and New Testaments, a man is bidden to cleave to his wife, not to a group. The Song of Songs celebrates the sexual bond of romance within marriage, an act whose ultimate power stems from its exclusivity: "Love is as strong as death, its jealousy unyielding as the grave. It burns like blazing fire, like a mighty flame." (Song of Songs 8:6–7). Solomon, who penned these inspired words, nonetheless fell prey to the same temptation to adultery that betook his father, David. Both paid terrible prices for it, as did their households and the nation of Israel, underscoring the fact that when God makes a point, it is wise to pay attention.

The Iowan quartet reportedly has been together three years, bonded by their common faith in Wicca, a pagan cult that worships nature instead of the Creator.

As for little Rowan, he will be watching, like Solomon, how his own father conducts himself. "Diversity is what humans are about," says Dawn as she explains that the group probably will relocate to a more cosmopolitan area for Rowan's sake. If he grows up here, he will have too narrow a view of what normal is—even with our family. That is, Rowan is jeopardized by being around too many Iowans who don't appreciate serial adultery. Better to get him to a city where he might learn new traditions. Say, somewhere like San Francisco or Madison, Wisconsin.

Periodical Bibliography

The following articles have been selected to supplement the diverse views presented in this chapter. Addresses are provided for periodicals not indexed in the *Readers' Guide to Periodical Literature*, the *Alternative Press Index*, the *Social Sciences Index*, or the *Index to Legal Periodicals and Books*.

Mark Clayton	"Prostitution 'Circuit' Takes Girls Across North America," *Christian Science Monitor*, August 23, 1996.
Ted Gideonse	"All Sex, All the Time," *Advocate*, May 26, 1998.
Issues and Controversies On File	"Prostitution," August 8, 1997. Available from Facts On File News Services, 11 Penn Plaza, New York, NY 10001-2006.
Holman W. Jenkins Jr.	"Porn Again? An Industry Fantasizes About Respect," *Wall Street Journal*, April 1, 1998.
David Kirby	"L.A. Confidential," *Poz*, April 1999. Available from 349 W. 12th St., New York, NY 10014-1721.
Elizabeth Larson	"Poly Sex for Beginners," *Utne Reader*, November/December 1998.
Wendy McElroy	"Whores vs. Feminists," *Liberty*, January 1999. Available from PO Box 1181, Port Townsend, WA 98368.
Ann E. Menasche	"An Interview with Diana Russell: Violence, Pornography, and Woman Hating," *Against the Current*, July/August 1997.
Rachel A. Roemhildt	"Americans Wouldn't Know It, But Pornography Is Illegal," *Insight*, December 14, 1998. Available from 3600 New York Ave. NE, Washington, DC 20002.
Robert Scheer	"The Dark Side of the New World Order," *Los Angeles Times*, January 13, 1998.
Lynn Snowden	"Deep Inside the Valley of Sin," *George*, March 1998. Available from 1633 Broadway, 41st Floor, New York, NY 10019.
Joel Stein	"Porn Goes Mainstream," *Time*, September 7, 1998.
Chitaporn Vanaspong	"Dangerous Chat," *Toward Freedom*, Winter 1998/1999.

For Further Discussion

Chapter 1

1. Teresa R. Wagner argues that America's acceptance of Alfred C. Kinsey's sex research contributed to a decline in sexual morality. John Bancroft contends that Kinsey's legacy has advanced the understanding of human sexuality. Wagner is affiliated with the Family Research Council, a conservative advocacy organization. Bancroft is the director of the Kinsey Institute in Sex, Gender, and Reproduction. Does knowing their backgrounds influence your assessment of their arguments? Explain your answer.

2. Kristina Sauerwein and Don Feder contend that a majority of youths engage in casual sex. Frederica Mathewes-Green maintains that a growing number of young people believe that nonmarital sex is wrong. What evidence do these authors present to support their conclusions? Whose argument is most persuasive? Why?

3. Roger Scruton claims that so-called sexual liberation has damaged American culture by allowing lust to eclipse commitment, love, and trust. Leonore Tiefer, on the other hand, argues that Americans are misinformed about sexuality and therefore lack a healthy perspective about sex and relationships. Whose viewpoint do you agree with, and why?

Chapter 2

1. Sarah E. Hinlicky argues that the power of a woman's decision to remain a virgin until marriage largely rests in her "refusal to exploit or be exploited." Valerie Gibson contends that women who advocate premarital abstinence often want to use their virginity as a "bargaining tool" in getting what they want from a man. In your opinion, is the resolution to abstain from premarital sex based on a refusal to be manipulative? Explain your answer.

2. Robyn Brown uses personal testimony to support her argument in favor of premarital cohabitation. David Popenoe and Barbara Dafoe Whitehead use national surveys and statistics to support their contention that couples should not live together before marriage. Whose rhetorical style is more convincing? Explain your answer, using examples from the viewpoints.

3. Donald DeMarco maintains that the use of contraception compromises the intimacy between husband and wife because it blocks the part of themselves that is intended for procreation.

Does James Nuechterlein's viewpoint effectively refute De-Marco's argument? Why or why not?

Chapter 3

1. Compare Carolyn Mackler's argument supporting comprehensive sex education programs with the National Coalition of Abstinence Education's defense of abstinence-centered curricula. In your opinion, which sex education curriculum should American public schools endorse? Why?

2. Mary Renee Smith maintains that information about masturbation should be included in sex education programs. How would Mona Charen respond to Smith's contention? Which author do you agree with, and why?

3. Beth Reis argues that teachers should actively fight against antigay prejudice by giving students accurate information about sexual orientation and encouraging respect for sexual minorities. William Norman Grigg contends that schools should not encourage acceptance of homosexuality because homosexual behavior is immoral and self-destructive. Do you believe that educational institutions should openly advocate acceptance of homosexuality? Why or why not? Support your answer with evidence from the viewpoints.

Chapter 4

1. Cite some of the evidence that Rosaline Bush uses to support her view that pornography is harmful. Do you find her evidence persuasive? If so, why? If not, what evidence provided by Nina Hartley do you find convincing?

2. Prior to reading this chapter, what did you assume would be the feminist stance on sex work and prostitution? Did the chapter change your understanding of the feminist viewpoint? Explain your response.

3. In their viewpoints, Alicia Potter and Robert H. Knight use stories from the Bible to help defend their support of polyamory or monogamy, respectively. What obstacles, if any, are there in choosing the Bible to promote either polyamory or monogamy?

Organizations to Contact

The editors have compiled the following list of organizations concerned with the issues debated in this book. The descriptions are derived from materials provided by the organizations. All have publications or information available for interested readers. The list was compiled on the date of publication of the present volume; the information provided here may change. Be aware that many organizations take several weeks or longer to respond to inquiries, so allow as much time as possible.

The Alan Guttmacher Institute
120 Wall St., New York, NY 10005
(212) 248-1111 • fax: (212) 248-1951
e-mail: info@agi-usa.org • website: http://www.agi-usa.org

The institute works to protect and expand the reproductive choices of all women and men. It strives to ensure that people have access to the information and services they need to exercise their rights and responsibilities concerning sexual activity, reproduction, and family planning. Among the institute's publications are the books *Teenage Pregnancy in Industrialized Countries* and *Today's Adolescents, Tomorrow's Parents: A Portrait of the Americas* and the report *Sex and America's Teenagers*.

Coalition for Positive Sexuality (CPS)
3712 N. Broadway, PMB #191, Chicago, IL 60613
(773) 604-1654
website: http://www.positive.org

The Coalition for Positive Sexuality is a grassroots direct-action group formed in the spring of 1992 by high school students and activists. CPS works to counteract the institutionalized misogyny, heterosexism, homophobia, racism, and ageism that students experience every day at school. It is dedicated to offering teens sexuality and safe sex education that is pro-woman, pro-lesbian/gay/bisexual, pro-safe sex, and pro-choice. Its motto is, "Have fun and be safe." CPS publishes the pamphlet *Just Say Yes*.

Eagle Forum
PO Box 618, Alton, IL 62002
(618) 462-5415 • fax: (618) 462-8909
e-mail: eagle@eagleforum.org • website: http://www.eagleforum.org

Eagle Forum, founded by conservative Phyllis Schlafly, advocates traditional family values. It stresses chastity before marriage and fidelity afterward, opposes birth control and abortion, and warns teens and others about the dangers of pornography and sexually transmitted diseases. The forum publishes the monthly *Phyllis Schlafly Report* as well as various brochures.

Family Research Council (FRC)
801 G St. NW, Washington, DC 20001
(202) 393-2100 • fax: (202) 393-2134
e-mail: corrdept@frc.org • website: http://www.frc.org

FRC is a research, resource, and education organization that promotes the traditional family. It advocates traditional family values in the media and educates citizens on how they can promote Judeo-Christian principles. The council publishes the weekly report *Ed Facts*, which analyzes breaking education news, and the bimonthly *Family Policy*, which seeks to strengthen family-centered institutions.

Focus on the Family
Colorado Springs, CO 80995
(719) 531-5181 • fax: (719) 531-3424
website: http://www.fotf.org

Focus on the Family is an organization that promotes Christian values and strong family ties and that campaigns against pornography and homosexual rights laws. It publishes the monthly magazine *Focus on the Family* and the books *Love Won Out: A Remarkable Journey Out of Homosexuality*, and *No Apologies . . . the Truth About Life, Love and Sex*.

IntiNet Resource Center
PO Box 4322, San Rafael, CA 94913
(415) 507-1739
e-mail: taj@LoveWithoutLimits.com
website: http://www.LoveWithoutLimits.com

IntiNet advocates the "expanded family," a number of adults who are members of a group marriage and who often share food, housing, and child rearing. Sexual relationships between the adults can be heterosexual or homosexual. IntiNet distributes information on the expanded family, which it believes will one day be the predominant lifestyle. It publishes the book *Love Without Limits: Responsible Nonmonogamy and the Quest for Sustainable Intimate Relationships* and the quarterly newsletter *Floodtide*.

Love in Action
PO Box 753307, Memphis, TN 38175
(901) 542-0250
e-mail: info@loveinaction.org
website: http://www.loveinaction.org

Love in Action is a ministry that believes that homosexuality is learned behavior and that all homosexual conduct is wrong because it violates God's laws. It provides support to gays and lesbians to help them convert to heterosexuality. Love in Action publishes articles on the causes of homosexuality, homosexuality and sin, sexual abuse, and other topics; testimonies from homosexuals and parents of gays; the books *A Step Further* and *Helping People Step Out of Homosexuality;* and the monthly newsletter *Lifelines.*

National Campaign to Prevent Teen Pregnancy
21 M St. NW, Ste. 300, Washington, DC 20037
(202) 261-5655
website: http://www.teenpregnancy.org

The mission of the National Campaign is to reduce teenage pregnancy by promoting values and activities that are consistent with a pregnancy-free adolescence. The campaign's goal is to reduce the pregnancy rate among teenage girls by one-third by the year 2005. The campaign publishes pamphlets, brochures, and opinion polls such as: *No Easy Answers: Research Finding on Programs to Reduce Teen Pregnancy*, *Not Just for Girls: Involving Boys and Men in Teen Pregnancy Prevention*, and *Public Opinion Polls and Teen Pregnancy.*

National Coalition Against Censorship (NCAC)
275 Seventh Ave., New York, NY 10001
(212) 807-6222 • fax: (212) 807-6245
e-mail: ncac@ncac.org • website: http://www.ncac.org

NCAC is an alliance of organizations committed to defending freedom of thought, inquiry, and expression by engaging in public education and advocacy on national and local levels. It believes censorship is dangerous because it represses intellectual and artistic freedom. NCAC maintains a library of information dealing with First Amendment issues and sponsors public meetings on these issues as well as special programs on countering censorship in public schools. It publishes the quarterly newsletter *Censorship News.*

National Coalition for the Protection of Children and Families
800 Compton Rd., Ste. 9224, Cincinnati, OH 45231
(513) 521-6227 • fax: (513) 521-6337
e-mail: ncpcf@eos.net • website: http://www.nationalcoalition.org

NCPCF works with civic, legal, and religious groups who seek to eliminate obscenity and adult and child pornography. It sponsors workshops and provides written, video, and audio materials about ways to campaign against pornography, sexual violence, and child victimization. Its publications include *Warning: What You Risk by Using Porn*, *Protecting Your Family in Cyberspace*, and the bimonthly newsletter *Standing Together*.

Parents, Families and Friends of Lesbians and Gays (P-FLAG)
1101 14th St. NW, Ste. 1030, Washington, DC 20005
(202) 638-4200 • fax: (202) 638-0243
e-mail: info@pflag.org • website: http://www.pflag.org
P-FLAG is a national organization that provides support and educational services for gays, lesbians, bisexuals, and their families and friends. It works to end prejudice and discrimination against homosexual and bisexual persons. It publishes and distributes booklets and papers, including *About Our Children*, *Coming Out to My Parents*, and *Why Is My Child Gay?*

Planned Parenthood Federation of America (PPFA)
810 Seventh Ave., New York, NY 10019
(212) 541-7800 • fax: (212) 245-1845
e-mail: communications@ppfa.org • website: http://www.ppfa.org
Planned Parenthood supports people who wish to make their own decisions about having children without governmental interference. It promotes comprehensive sex education and provides contraceptive counseling and services through clinics across the United States. Its publications include the brochures *Guide to Birth Control: Seven Accepted Methods of Contraception*, *Teensex? It's Okay to Say No Way*, and the bimonthly newsletter *LINK Line*.

Respect, Inc.
PO Box 349, Bradley, IL 60915-0349
(815) 932-8389
e-mail: sexrespect@lochrie.com
website: http://www.sexrespect.com
Respect, Inc. is the organization that developed Sex Respect, a sex education curriculum that stresses abstinence among teens. The curriculum teaches youths that abstaining from premarital sex is their right, is in society's best interest, and is in the spirit of true sexual freedom. *Everyone Is Not Doing It* is a video which promotes abstinence among high school students.

Sex Information and Education Council of Canada (SIECCAN)
850 Coxwell Ave., Toronto, Ontario, M4C 5R1 Canada
(416) 466-5304 • fax: (416) 778-0785
e-mail: sieccan@web.net • website: http://www.sieccan.org
SIECCAN conducts research on sexual health and sexuality education, publishes *The Canadian Journal of Human Sexuality* and the resource document *Common Questions About Sexual Health Education*, and maintains an information service for health professionals.

**Sexuality Information and Education
Council of the United States (SIECUS)**
130 W 42nd St., Ste. 350, New York, NY 10036-7802
(212) 819-9770 • fax: (212) 819-9776
e-mail: siecus@siecus.org • website: http://www.siecus.org
SIECUS is an organization of educators, physicians, social workers, and others who support the individual's right to acquire knowledge of sexuality and who encourage responsible sexual behavior. The council promotes comprehensive sex education for all children that includes AIDS education, teaching about homosexuality, and instruction about contraceptives and sexually transmitted diseases. Its publications include fact sheets, annotated bibliographies by topic, the booklet *Talk About Sex*, and the bimonthly *SIECUS Report*.

U.S. Public Health Service
200 Independence Ave. SW, Washington, DC 20201
(202) 619-0257
website: http://www.dhhs.gov/phs
The Public Health Service's mission is to promote the protection and advancement of the public's physical and mental health. Agencies within the service, such as the Centers for Disease Control and Prevention (CDC), the Food and Drug Administration (FDA), and the National Institutes of Health (NIH), conduct research on contraceptives and sexually transmitted diseases. Their data is available in publications such as the CDC's *Morbidity and Mortality Weekly Report* and the *FDA Consumer*.

Bibliography of Books

Elizabeth Rice Allgeier and Albert Richard Allgeier — *Sexual Interactions: Basic Understandings*. Boston: Houghton Mifflin, 1998.

Deborah M. Anapol — *Polyamory: The New Love Without Limits*. San Rafael, CA: Intinet Resource Center, 1997.

Johann Christoph Arnold — *A Plea for Purity*. Farmington, PA: Plough, 1998.

Eleanor Ayer — *It's Okay to Say No: Choosing Sexual Abstinence*. New York: Rosen, 1997.

Richard M. Baird and Stuart E. Rosenbaum, eds. — *Pornography: Private Right or Public Menace?* Amherst, NY: Prometheus, 1998.

Kathleen Barry — *The Prostitution of Sexuality*. New York: New York University Press, 1995.

Ellen Bass and Kate Kaufman — *Free Your Mind: The Book for Gay, Lesbian, and Bisexual Youth and Their Allies*. New York: HarperPerennial, 1996.

Ruth Bell — *Changing Bodies, Changing Lives: A Book for Teens on Sex and Relationships*. New York: Times Books, 1998.

Michael D. Benson — *Coping with Birth Control*. New York: Rosen, 1998.

Joani Blank, ed. — *First Person Sexual: Women and Men Write About Self-Pleasuring*. San Francisco: Down There, 1996.

Karen Bouris — *The First Time: What Parents and Teenage Girls Should Know About 'Losing Your Virginity.'* Berkeley: Conrari, 1995.

Susie Bright — *Susie Bright's Sexual State of the Union*. New York: Simon & Schuster, 1997.

Gary R. Brooks — *The Centerfold Syndrome: How Men Can Overcome Objectification and Achieve Intimacy with Women*. San Francisco: Jossey-Bass, 1995.

David Bull — *Cool and Celibate?: Sex and No Sex*. Boston: Element, 1998.

Lynn S. Chancer — *Reconcilable Differences: Confronting Beauty, Pornography, and the Future of Feminism*. Berkeley: University of California Press, 1998.

Harry M. Clor — *Public Morality and Liberal Society: Essays on Decency, Law, and Pornography*. Notre Dame, IN: University of Notre Dame Press, 1997.

Danielle Crittendon	*What Our Mothers Didn't Tell Us: Why Happiness Eludes the Modern Woman.* New York: Simon & Schuster, 1999.
Betty Dodson	*Sex for One: The Joy of Selfloving.* New York: Crown, 1996.
James Elias, Vern L. Bullough, and Veronica Elias, eds.	*Prostitution: On Whores, Hustlers, and Johns.* Amherst, NY: Prometheus, 1999.
Leland Elliott and Cynthia Brantley	*Sex on Campus: The Naked Truth About the Real Sex Lives of College Students.* New York: Random House, 1997.
Maggie Gallagher	*The Abolition of Marriage: How We Destroy Lasting Love.* Washington, DC: Regnery, 1996.
George Grant and Mark A. Horne	*Legislating Immorality: The Homosexual Movement Comes Out of the Closet.* Franklin, TN: Moody Press and Legacy Communications, 1993.
John Heidenry	*What Wild Ecstasy: The Rise and Fall of the Sexual Revolution.* New York: Simon & Schuster, 1997.
Loraine Hutchins and Lani Kaahumanu, eds.	*Bi Any Other Name: Bisexual People Speak Out.* Los Angeles: Alyson, 1991.
Janet Shibley Hyde and John D. Delamater	*Understanding Human Sexuality.* Boston: McGraw-Hill, 1996.
Richard A. Isay	*Becoming Gay: The Journey to Self-Acceptance.* New York: Henry Holt, 1997.
Raymond Jamiolkowski	*A Baby Doesn't Make the Man: Alternative Sources of Power and Manhood for Young Men.* New York: Rosen, 1997.
James Howard Jones	*Alfred C. Kinsey: A Public/Private Life.* New York: W.W. Norton, 1997.
Jane Juffer	*At Home with Pornography: Women, Sex, and Everyday Life.* New York: New York University Press, 1998.
Wendy Kaminer	*True Love Waits: Essays and Criticism.* New York: Perseus, 1997.
Kevin Kelly	*New Directions in Sexual Ethics: Moral Theology and the Challenge of AIDS.* London: Cassell Academic, 1999.
Bruce M. King	*Human Sexuality Today.* Upper Saddle River, NJ: Prentice Hall, 1999.
Jon Knowles and Marcia Ringel	*All About Birth Control: A Personal Guide.* New York: Three Rivers Press, 1998.
Tim F. LaHaye and Beverly LaHaye	*The Act of Marriage: The Beauty of Sexual Love.* Grand Rapids, MI: Zondervan, 1998.

Ronald David Lawler et al. — *Catholic Sexual Ethics: A Summary, Explanation, and Defense*. Huntington, IN: Our Sunday Visitor, 1998.

E. James Lieberman and Karen Lieberman Troccoli — *Like It Is: A Teen Sex Guide*. Jefferson, NC: McFarland, 1998.

Nan Bauer Maglin and Donna Perry, eds. — *'Bad Girls'/'Good Girls': Women, Sex, and Power in the Nineties*. Piscataway, NJ: Rutgers University Press, 1996.

Adam Mastoon — *The Shared Heart: Portraits and Stories Celebrating Lesbian, Gay, and Bisexual Young People*. New York: William Morrow, 1997.

Tara McCarthy — *Been There, Haven't Done That: A Virgin's Memoir*. New York: Warner Books, 1998.

Wendy McElroy — *XXX: A Woman's Right to Pornography*. New York: St. Martin's Press, 1995.

Michael Medved and Diane Medved — *Saving Childhood: Protecting Our Children from the National Assault on Innocence*. New York: HarperCollins, 1998.

John Money — *Sin, Science, and the Sex Police*. Amherst, NY: Prometheus, 1999.

James B. Nelson — *Between Two Gardens: Reflections on Sexuality and Religious Experience*. Cleveland: Pilgrim Press, 1997.

Jeffrey S. Nevid — *Choices: Sex in the Age of STDs*. Needham Heights, MD: Allyn and Bacon, 1997.

Maggie Paley — *The Book of the Penis*. New York: Grove, 1999.

Richard A. Panzer — *Condom Nation: Blind Faith, Bad Science*. Westwood, NJ: Center for Educational Media, 1997.

Cindy Patton — *Fatal Advice: How Safe-Sex Education Went Wrong*. Durham, NC: Duke University Press, 1996.

Adam Phillips — *Monogamy*. New York: Pantheon Books, 1996.

Malcolm Potts and Roger Short — *Ever Since Adam: The Evolution of Human Sexuality*. New York: Cambridge University Press, 1999.

Igor Primoratz — *Ethics and Sex*. New York: Routledge, 1999.

Judith A. Reisman — *Kinsey: Crimes & Consequences the Red Queen & the Grand Scheme*. Crestwood, KY: Institute for Media Education, 1998.

Ira L. Reiss and Harriet M. Reiss — *Solving America's Sexual Crises*. Amherst, NY: Prometheus, 1997.

Martin Rimm

Pornographer's Handbook: How to Exploit Women, Dupe Men, and Make Lots of Money. Pittsburgh: Carnegie Mellon University Press, 1995.

Katie Roiphe

Last Night in Paradise: Sex and Morals at the Century's End. Boston: Little, Brown & Company, 1997.

Pepper Schwartz and Virginia Rutter

The Gender of Sexuality. Thousand Oaks, CA: Pine Forge Press, 1998.

Wendy Shalit

A Return to Modesty: Discovering the Lost Virtue. New York: Free Press, 1999.

Alan Soble, ed.

The Philosophy of Sex. Lanham, MD: Rowman & Littlefield, 1997.

Charles W. Socarides

Homosexuality: A Freedom Too Far. Phoenix: Adam Margrave Books, 1995.

Nadine Strossen

Defending Pornography: Free Speech, Sex, and the Fight for Women's Rights. New York: Scribner, 1995.

Andrew Sullivan

Virtually Normal: An Argument About Homosexuality. New York: Knopf, 1995.

Bonnie Eaker Weil et al.

Adultery: The Forgivable Sin. Norwalk, CT: Hastings House, 1994.

Naomi Wolf

Promiscuities: The Secret Struggle for Womanhood. New York: Random House, 1997.

Edwin H. Young

Pure Sex. Sisters, OR: Multnomah, 1997.

Malik Yusef, ed.

Am I the Last Virgin?: Ten African American Reflections on Sex and Love. London: Aladdin Paperbacks, 1997.

Index

.